MARINE
ANTIQUES

BOOKS BY MARIAN KLAMKIN

Flower Arrangements That Last
Flower Arranging for Period Decoration
The Collector's Book of Boxes
The Collector's Book of Wedgwood
The Collector's Book of Art Nouveau
The Collector's Book of Bottles
Hands to Work: Shaker Folk Art and Industries
White House China
American Patriotic and Political China
The Return of Lafayette
The Collector's Guide to Depression Glass
Depression Glass Collector's Price Guide
Wood Carvings: North American Folk Sculptures (*with Charles Klamkin*)
Investing in Antiques and Popular Collectibles (*with Charles Klamkin*)
The Collector's Guide to Carnival Glass
Old Sheet Music: A Pictorial History of the Cover Art and Design
Picture Postcards
Marine Antiques

MARINE ANTIQUES

Marian Klamkin

Illustrated with photographs by Charles Klamkin

DODD, MEAD & COMPANY · NEW YORK

Library of Congress Cataloging in Publication Data

Klamkin, Marian.
 Marine antiques.

 Bibliography: p.
 Includes index.
 1. Nautical paraphernalia—Collectors and
collecting. I. Title.
V745.K56   623.8′075   75-29437
ISBN 0-396-07225-9

For Peter

ACKNOWLEDGMENTS

I deeply appreciate the help and co-operation I received from Norman Flayderman, writer, collector and dealer in the field of marine antiques. Mr. Flayderman not only allowed his private collection to be photographed, but also gave freely of his time and knowledge.

Mr. Sterling D. Emerson, director, Shelburne Museum, Shelburne, Vermont, and his staff were also most generous in sharing research materials and providing objects to be photographed. I would also like to thank Mr. Walter B. Stearns, curator of the Suffolk County Whaling Museum, Sag Harbor, New York, for allowing photographs to be taken of the collection under his care.

Mr. George D. Wintress of The Seamen's Bank for Savings of New York was most helpful in sending photographs and information from the bank's superb collection of ship models.

CONTENTS

ILLUSTRATIONS IN COLOR

Following page 116, including the following subjects:

Ship's bell
"Sow's ears" (painted leaves)
"Sailor's Return," "Sailor's Farewell " (color prints)
"Sailor's Valentine" (Barbados shellwork)
Embroidered jumper
Ship embroidered in wool
Engraved shell
Figurehead from the ship *Bosphorus*
Valentine made by British sailor
Chinese porcelain
Beaker with enameled naval scene
Hand-painted jug
Hand-painted plate with picture of sailor and lady
Elsinore hand-painted bowl
Anchor Line advertising card
"The Sperm Whale in a Flurry" (color print)
Goblet commemorating a launching

1

INTRODUCTION

The history of man's life on the sea transgresses all national boundaries and goes back to the beginning of civilization. It involves hundreds of battles, the exploration of new continents and the interchange of goods among the countries of the world. It tells of the provision of food and other products that seagoing nations have taken from the oceans, and relates to us the meaning of gold and other treasures to be taken from faraway places. It is the saga of civilization's quest for a better way of life—and the often tragic results of that search. While many men took to the sea to look for riches, others used the sea to transport humans for the purpose of enslaving them.

The mysteries of the sea have been the subject of myths and legends, superstition and prejudice, poetry and songs. The sea is a distinct category of literature and has created national heroes for all countries engaged in seafaring. It also created its own breed of men, some remembered for their goodwill in connection with their lives aboard ship and many more known for their infamous deeds. The infamous make better stories.

The bodies of water that cover two-thirds of the earth's surface have yielded unlimited riches to mankind. It has only recently been discovered that perhaps we have taken too much and have been careless in our use of this bounty. The once plentiful sea creatures are struggling to survive due to the greed of men who plundered the ocean in search of food and the valuable products found in the carcass of the whale and the fur-bearing sea animals. As improvements were made in fishing vessels, we became more careless concerning the ocean's riches.

A great many sailing ships ended their days beneath the waters they had sailed. With improved diving methods and the development of the science of marine archeology, it is evident that a great deal of new information will be added to what we already know of the early sailing vessels. This information will be extremely helpful to marine historians and should aid in dating many of the nautical artifacts now in collections all over the world.

The romantic aspects of the days of the sailing ship become stronger as we move farther and farther away from the time when sails were the only means of propelling a ship across the ocean. Few artists exposed to the sight of a ship in full sail have been able to avoid attempting to put this magnificent picture on canvas. Marine paintings range in quality from the fine work of the world's most outstanding artists to that of the Sunday painter fortunate enough to have spent a day or two at the seashore. Sea paintings are a category of marine art that has enjoyed too long a life and too much variety to be discussed here. However, the same feelings that inspired the great artists to record the appearance of thousands of sailing ships also led to the decoration of many other objects of a collectible nature. Just as artists painted the portrait of a ship to order for its master, so decorators of pottery and porcelain painted or printed nautical designs on objects that they sold to sailors who wanted a remembrance of the ship on which they had sailed.

The category of marine antiques is an enormous one and is, of course, international in style and scope. Sailors visiting foreign ports exchanged ideas with seafarers of other nations, and many motifs and techniques in sailor-made arts and crafts were adapted. Land-bound art and architecture developed along national or regional styles, but seafaring men were always quick to note innovations and changes that led to faster or more seaworthy craft and to attempt any handicraft to which they were exposed.

In their own folk art, as well as the objects that were made to be sold to them in the ports of the world, sailors have long been aware of the designs and motifs that best represent their particular vocation and surroundings. Anchors, ship's wheels, the compass rose, lighthouses, ships and the figure of the sailor have been used as decoration on objects made of pottery, porcelain, glass, wood, textiles and metal. Sailors were always good customers for these souvenir items. When a picture of their own ship could quickly be painted on a bowl or cup, the merchant in port had a quick sale. Most of these items

G R

All Dashing High-spirited
YOUNG HEROES

Who wish to obtain GLORY in the SERVICE
of their Country, have now the finest Opportunity,
by entering that enterprizing respectable Corps

THE ROYAL
MARINES.

Every one must be well aware, that this Honorable Corps, possesses Advantages superior to any other under the Crown. Good Quarters whilst on Shore; on Board, plenty of Beef, Pudding, and Wine after Dinner. Even these Advantages are trifling when compared to the inestimable one

PRIZE MONEY.

Remember the Galloons; when the Private Marine made sufficient Prize Money to render himself and Family comfortable for Life.

Remember these Times may return, it is impossible to say how soon.

Loose no Time! therefore, in repairing to the head Quarters of the 1st Lieu. H. B. MENDS, of the Plymouth Division of Royal Marines, commanded by Lieu. Gen. BRIGHT, or to *Serjeant GREBBLE*, at the *BLUE BOWL, PITHAY, BRISTOL*, where every attention will be paid to them.

Eleven Guineas Bounty
SEVEN YEARS SERVICE.
Sixteen Guineas
UNLIMITTED SERVICE.

Boys 5 Feet, *Eight Guineas*, limitted Service. *Twelve Pounds*, unlimited.

NOW OR NEVER, ENGLAND FOREVER.

✱ The Bringers of Recruits will be handsomely rewarded.

GOD SAVE the KING.

Poster for recruiting Royal Marines. Height seemed more important than age.
FLAYDERMAN COLLECTION

were probably sold to ship's officers or to the sailor who had a family back home.

The deepwater merchant sailors and navy men of the nineteenth century, on the whole, dedicated their lives to the sea. The majority of seafaring men had few or no ties with anyone outside of their fellow crew members. They signed on a ship at an early age, usually around twelve or thirteen, and spent the remainder of their lives as sailors. If they were ambitious or had some family influence, they became masters of their own ships in their early twenties. In America it was not unusual for a man of nineteen to have charge of a ship, especially if members of his family had an interest in the vessel.

The merchant sailor was a breed unlike men in any other vocation, and he often lost his national identity. His preference for sign-

3

Sailors' Homes existed in most of the large ports of the world and were often the only home a seagoing man knew. FLAYDERMAN COLLECTION

ing on a particular vessel had more to do with the quality of the food and the reputation of the ship's master than with the ship's country of origin. If conditions were especially unpleasant on a voyage out, a sailor would feel no compunction about jumping ship as soon as the opportunity arose. He often had no ties and no family, and in every major port in the world he was aware of the location of a sailors' home where he could eat, drink and sleep until he signed on for another voyage. His pay was low and was usually spent on drink as soon as a ship reached port.

A merchant seaman's life was hard and he aged quickly. When he didn't meet an early death from accident or disease, he ended his days in a home for sailors. Few were literate, but for the ordinary seaman reading and writing were unnecessary skills. All time spent aboard a merchant ship belonged to the shipping company, and a sailor expected to be driven hard by his master. His worldly goods had to fit into a seabag and chest, and his most prized possessions were his needles, palm, a hunk of beeswax, a fid, a spike and the ever-present sharp knife.

Obviously, there was little time for arts and crafts aboard the fast clippers that journeyed around Cape Horn in the latter half of the nineteenth century, and it is unlikely that much of the sailor folk art that exists today came from that period. The masters of these ships were notoriously hard-driving and dictatorial, and their only object was to cut as much time as possible from their journey. As trade became more competitive, crews were reduced to a minimum, and the work was unremitting and grueling.

More and more fast ships were built to accommodate the gold-seeking American Easterners and the Europeans who headed for California and Australia. Consequently, it became more difficult to find adequate crews to man the clippers. Ship's masters used any means available to gather their crews, and a sailor who drank himself into a stupor while in port did so at his own risk. It was not unusual

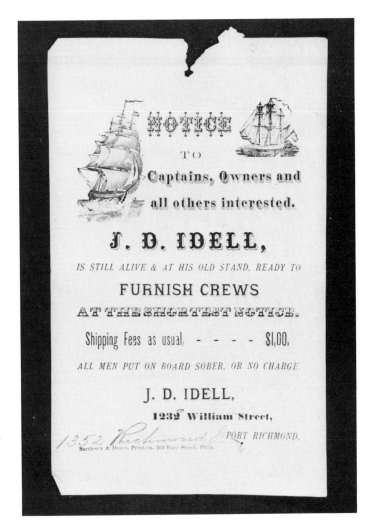

Brokers furnished crew members for merchant vessels in the nineteenth century. FLAYDERMAN COLLECTION

for him to wake up on board a strange ship headed "'round the Horn." If he were fortunate enough to find himself on one with decent food and a good master, he usually accepted his lot and carried a grudge only against the "broker" who, at a dollar a head, did a good business in furnishing crews. If circumstances on board were not acceptable to the shanghaied sailor, he jumped ship at the first opportunity.

It was mostly on the whaling vessels of the late eighteenth and nineteenth centuries that sailors found time to express themselves in a variety of crafts. As these ships were forced to go farther and

Left: The toggle harpoon, invented by the black American blacksmith Lewis Temple in 1848, was a great improvement over earlier designs. SUFFOLK COUNTY WHALING MUSEUM

Below: Inefficient design of early harpoons resulted in many whales being lost after contact had been made. SUFFOLK COUNTY WHALING MUSEUM

Trying-out pots of iron were used for cooking whale blubber on board ship to extract precious oil. SUFFOLK COUNTY WHALING MUSEUM

farther from their home ports in search of the lucrative whale, the voyages out were a time of preparation for the catch. Once in the whaling grounds, there was little to do but wait until the time when a whale was sighted. During these long periods of intense boredom, the sailor's knife and needle were put to work fashioning designs on whalebone and wood. Although not confined solely to American whalemen, the art of scrimshaw was widely practiced among them, and the results have become known as an indigenous American folk art. British sailors, also adept with knife and needle, made woolen "paintings" with nautical motifs and engaged in other crafts as well.

A sailing man who could read and write often used his spare time on board ship writing and sometimes profusely illustrating a journal. As will be discussed later, these journals give us a rather graphic picture of life on a sailing ship. Although important historically, they were also of value to the writer in that they helped him to keep a perspective of himself and his fellows. One sailor, Benjamin C. Townsend, on his second East India voyage in 1848, added a post-script to his journal upon his return home that summarized his voyage and the value to him of keeping this record:

Many an unexpected change has taken place during the past 8 months. Many an old acquaintance *dead* and buried. Few married. But it is a blessing to me (if not finding all my relations at home) to know they are alive and well and everything looking so cheerfully at home. This is my parting writing in this log. It has served me well. Had many a ducking, many a pounding and withall a severe toss now and then in some obscure corner of a *sailors cabin*, but like a faithful servant it [the journal] has staid by me to the last.

The list of provisions for a whaling voyage was filled in by the ship's captain. FLAYDERMAN COLLECTION

Provision lists were given away by waterfront merchants to potential customers. FLAYDERMAN COLLECTION

It shan't go now for sartain bekase I'll keep it for the good it has done.

—Benjamin C. Townsend

Although collectors of marine antiques search for examples of the mariners' art and then for relics that are all that remain of the old sailing ships, many other marine-related objects are available and are part of the entire story of the sailing-ship era. Seaport towns catered to the needs of shipowners and sailors. These towns were often the only link with land that a sailing man had, and most of the business of seaports related to the ships that sailed in and out of port and the men who made up their crews. Souvenirs were made that would appeal to sailors, and these all had some motif of the ship or sea as decoration. Shaving mugs and cups were quickly painted to order with the name of the ship's master and a portrait of his ship. Since ships remained in some ports several months waiting for crops to ripen or cargo to be loaded, there was often time for portraits to be painted or decorative objects to be made to order.

Advertisement for passengers, trade cards announcing the goods and services available to a ship's master by local merchants, trade signs and supply booklets that still survive are all evidence that every aspect of the shipping business was highly competitive in the nineteenth century. When a ship put into port after a lengthy journey, an entire town became active in searching for at least a portion of the business that it brought.

There were times, however, when businessmen on shore had few scruples in their attempts to make money from the shipping business. When thousands of starving Irishmen migrated to the port of Liverpool on their way to America during the potato famine of 1847, many citizens of Liverpool were eager to take the last remaining money these people owned by renting them damp cellars and providing inadequate food while they waited for passage on a crowded ship. In this situation the shipowners were also less than upright, providing the emigrants with accommodations that were inhuman enough to make Ireland look like paradise. Masters of slave ships were only a little more thoughtful concerning the well-being of their cargo, since there was money to be made only if it arrived in good health. Once an emigrant had paid for his passage, many shipowners—both American and British—cared little whether these particular passengers lived through the voyage.

9

w

In CONGRESS,
WEDNESDAY, APRIL 3, 1776.

INSTRUCTIONS to the COMMANDERS of Private Ships or Vessels of War, which shall have Commissions or Letters of Marque and Reprisal, authorising them to make Captures of British Vessels and Cargoes.

I.

YOU may, by Force of Arms, attack, subdue, and take all Ships and other Vessels belonging to the Inhabitants of Great Britain, on the High Seas, or between high-water and low-water Marks, except Ships and Vessels bringing Persons who intend to settle and reside in the United Colonies, or bringing Arms, Ammunition or Warlike Stores to the said Colonies, for the Use of such Inhabitants thereof as are Friends to the American Cause, which you shall suffer to pass unmolested, the Commanders thereof permitting a peaceable Search, and giving satisfactory Information of the Contents of the Ladings, and Destinations of the Voyages.

II.

You may, by Force of Arms, attack, subdue, and take all Ships and other Vessels whatsoever carrying Soldiers, Arms, Gun-powder, Ammunition, Provisions, or any other contraband Goods, to any of the British Armies or Ships of War employed against these Colonies.

III.

You shall bring such Ships and Vessels as you shall take, with their Guns, Rigging, Tackle, Apparel, Furniture and Ladings, to some convenient Port or Ports of the United Colonies, that Proceedings may thereupon be had in due Form before the Courts which are or shall be there appointed to hear and determine Causes civil and maritime.

IV.

You or one of your Chief Officers shall bring or send the Master and Pilot and one or more principal Person or Persons of the Company of every Ship or Vessel by you taken, as soon after the Capture as may be, to the Judge or Judges of such Court as aforesaid, to be examined upon Oath, and make Answer to the Interrogatories which may be propounded touching the Interest or Property of the Ship or Vessel and her Lading; and at the same Time you shall deliver or cause to be delivered to the Judge or Judges, all Passes, Sea Briefs, Charter Parties, Bills of Lading, Cockets Letters, and other Documents and Writings found on Board, proving the said Papers by the Affidavit of yourself, or of some other Person present at the Capture, to be produced as they were received, without Fraud, Addition, Subduction, or Embezzlement.

V.

You shall keep and preserve every Ship or Vessel and Cargo by you taken, until they shall by Sentence of a Court properly authorised be adjudged lawful Prize, not selling, spoiling, wasting, or diminishing the same or breaking the Bulk thereof, nor suffering any such Thing to be done.

VI.

If you, or any of your Officers or Crew shall, in cold Blood, kill or maim, or by Torture or otherwise, cruelly, inhumanly, and contrary to common Usage and the Practice of civilized Nations in War, treat any Person or Persons surprized in the Ship or Vessel you shall take, the Offender shall be severely punished.

VII.

You shall, by all convenient Opportunities, send to Congress written Accounts of the Captures you shall make, with the Number and Names of the Captives, Copies of your Journal from Time to Time, and Intelligence of what may occur or be discovered concerning the Designs of the Enemy, and the Destinations, Motions, and Operations of their Fleets and Armies.

VIII.

One Third, at the least, of your whole Company shall be Land Men.

IX.

You shall not ransome any Prisoners or Captives, but shall dispose of them in such Manner as the Congress, or if that be not sitting in the Colony whither they shall be brought, as the General Assembly, Convention, or Council or Committee of Safety of such Colony shall direct.

X.

You shall observe all such further Instructions as Congress shall hereafter give in the Premises, when you shall have Notice thereof.

XI.

If you shall do any Thing contrary to these Instructions, or to others hereafter to be given, or willingly suffer such Thing to be done, you shall not only forfeit your Commission, and be liable to an Action for Breach of the Condition of your Bond, but be responsible to the Party grieved for Damages sustained by such Mal-versation.

By Order of CONGRESS.

JOHN HANCOCK, President.

Broadside giving Congressional approval to American privateers and authorizing them to capture British vessels and cargoes. FLAYDERMAN COLLECTION

Document signed by James Madison and James Monroe authorizing the ship Piper *to act as a privateer in 1812.*
FLAYDERMAN COLLECTION

In surviving marine antiques can be found the history of the American Revolution, the Napoleonic Wars, the War of 1812 and the fascinating period of the privateers. Old documents, letters of marque, awards, logs and journals tell us a great deal of this period in history when governments presented shipowners with legal licenses to steal and plunder. One has only to study the journal of some unfortunate sailor who was taken prisoner and placed upon a foreign ship to realize that this indignity, while wholly resented, was also expected in the period at the end of the eighteenth century and the beginning of the nineteenth.

As the sailing ships were gradually replaced with steam-powered vessels, there was little thought given to preserving examples of the different types until it was too late. One of the most beautiful ships of the nineteenth century, the American extreme clipper ship, is now truly a ghost vessel. Not one example has survived, and it is only through models, paintings and prints that we have some idea of the grace of these sleek ships. One of the last American clippers, the *Benjamin Packard*, ended her days as a nightclub anchored off the shores of Long Island, and finally met her end in the 1938 hurricane that ripped the eastern shore of the United States. The *Cutty Sark* is the only remaining British clipper ship that has survived, and she is now on permanent display beside the Thames at Greenwich. The rebuilt *Constitution*, a frigate that played an important role in American sea history, is now a monument on display in the Boston Navy Yard. The whaler *C. W. Morgan* and the *Joseph Conrad* have been preserved at Mystic Seaport, a restoration in Connecticut. More will be said later about the concerted efforts in many countries around the world to preserve what is left of marine antiquities.

Business cards of waterfront brokers and suppliers. Merchants were competitive and active in soliciting business in every seaport town in the world. FLAYDERMAN COLLECTION

12

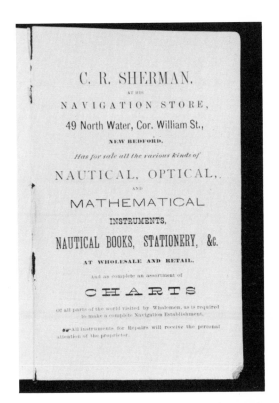

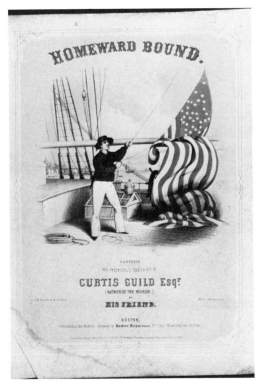

Left: Booklets like this one were handed out to American shipowners, who gave them to their captains for use when ordering supplies for a voyage. FLAYDERMAN COLLECTION
Right: Patriotic engraving for the song, "Homeward Bound." FLAYDERMAN COLLECTION

What remains of the great sailing-ship era are mostly the bits and pieces of ships that have found their way into private collections, historical societies, dealers' inventories and museums. Shipbuilder's models, carefully preserved by some governments and ignored by others, can still be found, as can the less accurate ship models made by seamen and hobbyists. Paintings and prints still survive in some quantity. Little attention has been given, however, to the many other nautical objects related to the sailing ships. Much of the ephemeral paper material that serves as a primary source of information for researchers and collectors has been lost through the years, but a few of the existing documents have been illustrated here.

The category of marine antiques transcends many other fields of collecting. Collectors of stamps, coins, medals, weaponry, ceramics, glass, maps, historical documents and native folk art are all familiar with some of the marine-related material that can be found within their specialties. However, the objects with nautical motifs or associations that can be found within these categories are only a part of what is still available. The true collector of marine antiques finds enormous satisfaction and a vicarious excitement in the material that relates only to ships and to the men who sailed them. He is an historian first and a collector second. He knows that, born in another era, he would have been a seafarer.

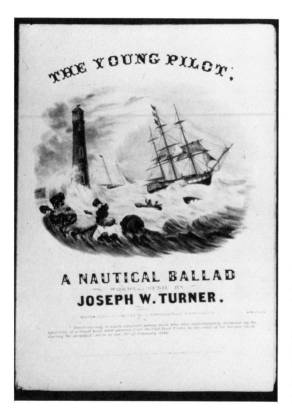

Engraved title page for "A Young Pilot," a nautical ballad. FLAYDERMAN COLLECTION

British naval officer's swordbelt and buckle, worn through Victorian era up to World War I. Centered in the wreath design is the Admiralty foul anchor. FLAYDERMAN COLLECTION

2
SHIP LOGS AND
SAILORS' JOURNALS

One of the most important types of source material, and therefore the most desirable of all collector's items for the marine historian, is the logbook or journal kept by all sea captains and some other officers or sailors while aboard ship. A great many logs and journals of the sailing-ship era are now in public museums and libraries. However, there are still some in private hands, and when a particularly desirable specimen comes up for sale it is an occasion for great excitement in the marine antiques world.

The logbooks and journals of the eighteenth and nineteenth centuries have become the ultimate collector's item in the field of marine antiques. In America there is a particularly high demand for whaling logbooks. These are official records of the voyage, the weather and the catch. While they are often not very exciting, the pages contain daily entries of whales sighted, lost or caught, and they are embellished with stamped whale shapes. Some of the early whaling logbooks have drawings of whales and ships sighted.

The mate on a whaling ship was responsible for keeping the log, and because they were official documents rather than personal recordings of a voyage, the majority of whaling logs are most often a record of the weather and resultant activities on shipboard. "First part of this day light winds from the SW. Ship under all sail cruising to the WNW at Sundown took in sail the latter part light winds from the SW. Made all sail Saw Sperm W. [hale] Lowered & Chased all day but did not strike Whale going to the E by N So Ends."

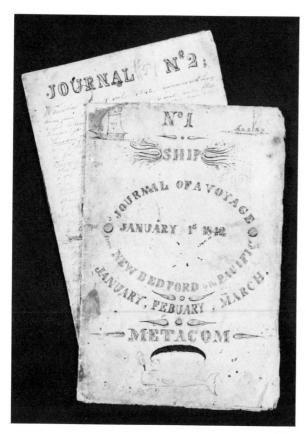

Left: Covers and titlepages of sea journals and logs were often carefully drawn and decorated. This is a two-volume journal of an 1842 whaling voyage out of New Bedford, Massachusetts. FLAYDERMAN COLLECTION

Right: Whales sighted, lost or caught were all recorded in journals and logs by means of inked stamps or small drawings. (Log of bark Nimrod, *1835.)* SUFFOLK COUNTY WHALING MUSEUM

Below: Titlepage of whaling log with typically fancy calligraphy as practiced by many log-keepers. SUFFOLK COUNTY WHALING MUSEUM

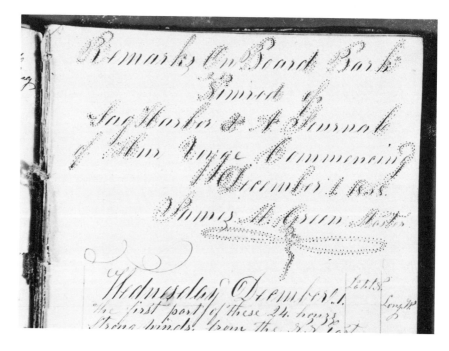

Lat. by obs 31.40 S Long by chr 45.12 W

Wednesday March 28th

First part of this day light winds from the S W
Ship under all sail Cruising to the N N W at
Sundown took in sail the latter part light winds from
the S W Made all sail saw Sperm W Lowered &
Chased all day but did not Strike Whale going
to the E by N So Ends

Lat by obs 31.00 S Long by chr 45.00 W

Thursday March 29th

First part of this day light winds & Calms Ship under
all sail Cruising to the N E at Sundown took in
Sail the latter part made all sail at 7 P M saw
a shoal of small Sperm Whale lowered & each
Boat struck & killed a Whale & took them
to the Ship one large Merchant Ship in
Sight So Ends

Lat by obs 30.18 S Long by chr 45.18 W

Friday March 30th

W. B.

S B

L B

Stowed Down 24 bbls

This records a dull and unproductive day aboard the bark *Nimrod*, which sailed out of Sag Harbor, Long Island, on December 1, 1858. The entry was made on March 28, 1859. The following day was somewhat more rewarding for the ship: "First part of this day light winds and calms. Ship under all sail cruising at the NE at Sundown took in sail the latter part made all sail. At 7 p.m. saw a shoal of small Sperm Whale Lowered & each boat struck and killed a

17

Whale & took theirs to the ship. One large merchant ship in sight. So ends.''

Whaling logs were kept in a variety of types of ledger books, but the long, narrow, lined books are the most common. While writing creativity of the log-keeper was discouraged, the title pages are often artistically drawn and lettered. Frequently small vignettes have been drawn of the ship or a whale, but on many title pages there is only a record of the voyage, the ship and its master.

While the whaling logs make rather boring reading to most collectors of general nautical material, the whaling buff uses his imagination to fill in the daily activities on the long and tedious journeys. To the whaling historian the reading of a ship's log can be as exciting as his first reading of *Moby Dick*. If the days appear to be lengthy and boring throughout such a log, the whaling historian is aware that such was the lot of the men who undertook the voyages, which often lasted as long as two or three years. One can easily understand why there was plenty of time for whaling men to pursue the art of scrimshaw aboard ship. One can turn the pages of a whaling ship's log for weeks at a time and not see one whale stamp, indicating that there was little for the men to do.

In connection with the whaling logs are the stamps used to record in them the whales sighted, lost, or caught. A whale's flukes indicate an unsuccessful chase. The stamp of a whole whale means a successful kill, but a whale's carcass recorded vertically in the log indicates the disappointment of a strike where the carcass had sunk. Some log-keepers were content to use the unadorned stamp; a few creative writers embellished the image with red ink to indicate blood where the whale was struck or a bloody spout.

The dies used to record the whales range from primitive hand-

Left: Whale stamp made of carved whalebone. SUFFOLK COUNTY WHALING MUSEUM *Right: Metal whale stamp with wood base.* SUFFOLK COUNTY WHALING MUSEUM

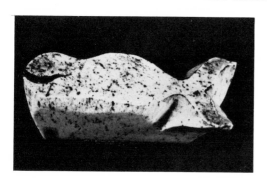

Metal whale stamp attached to cork. SUFFOLK COUNTY WHALING MUSEUM

carved, cartoonlike shapes to the very realistic whale outline. The most desirable of all whale dies are those hand carved from whalebone. However, the carved wood or metal dies are also now in high demand.

Of greater interest to the collector and historian than the official whaling logs are the personal journals of their voyages kept by whalemen. Since these records are unofficial, they often contain information concerning the life aboard ship as well as the personal philosophy and emotions of the writer. Frequently they were decorated with small drawings and paintings of crew members, their activities, and ships sighted.

Few members of any whaling crew could read or write, and it is probable that most of the unofficial journals were written by men who could look forward to shipping as first mate and eventually master aboard a whaling vessel. In some cases it is probable that keeping a journal was a way of passing time much as a complicated work of whalebone carving might be.

Most whaler's journals follow a format similar to the official logs. Each day's entry begins with data most pertinent to the well-being of a whaling man: the recording of wind direction and weather. Following this, however, there are often expressions of the journalist's feelings, which give us some insight into the life aboard a whaler and the welcome change of reaching a port.

Although some people search for whaling logs and journals, the true marine antiques collector is aware of the vast store of information in journals kept by men on any sailing vessel. Journals exist in all the languages of the countries that participated in ocean travel, and many are important as personal documents of the naval wars at the beginning of the nineteenth century or earlier. The history of

Journal extract illustrating the elevation of the St. Felix Islands. FLAYDERMAN COLLECTION

early maritime trade is also recorded in the journals of sailing ships.

In the earliest journals can be found geographical and navigational information that was of extreme importance to ships that might follow a particular route traveled by the vessel whose journey is recorded. Included in some of the journals of merchant seamen are drawings of the rock formations of small islands and the journalist's amateur account of how these islands were formed. One such description, with pen-and-ink drawings of the elevation of the Islands of St Felix, reads:

A fine breese, the *Islands* of "St Felix" is in sight—bearing N.N.W. 8 miles distant from the ship—9 A.M. the Capt. & 2nd Mate lowered their boats & made for the land on a fishing excursion. The Islands are all rocks—not a sign of vegetation or herbage to be seen upon them—Large numbers of *Seals* were seen—there is two stone houses in one of the *Islands* built by the sealers. . . ."

It is easy to understand that the keeper of this journal would have liked to have been included in the "fishing excursion." But he spent his time aboard ship recording from a distance the appearance of the islands and his opinion of them. On the same day he notes, "the boats returns to the Ship & brought us quite a mess of fish & a dozen or two

Diagram of how to splice a jibboom and an elevation showing the rock formation of an island sighted. FLAYDERMAN COLLECTION

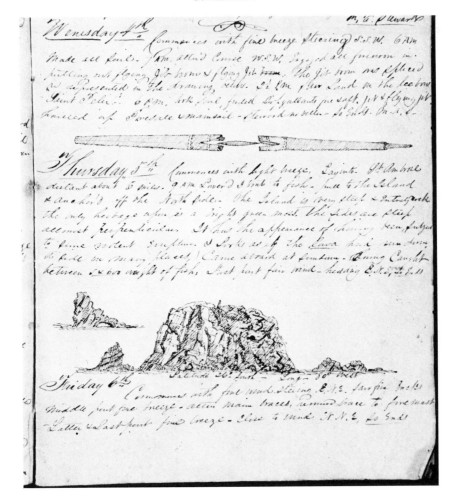

of Crabs." This journal is full of information, diagrams and drawings of helpful hints for the seaman who might have read it following this journey. A diagram of a blacksmith's forge set up aboard ship is described by its artist with enthusiasm: "Such a forge was never seen—" After the journalist was "engaged all forenoon in putting out flying jib boom & flying jib," he thoughtfully recorded his method of splicing the jib boom in a carefully drawn diagram.

A geological observation is recorded along with an elevation of the island of St Ambrose, which the sailor describes as "very steep & entirely rock, the only herbage upon it is a bright green moss. The sides are steep, almost perpendicular. It has the appearance of having been subject to some violent eruption. It looks like the *lava* had run down the side in many places." That the journalist was allowed to explore the island and to take a boat on a fishing excursion indicates that he was probably third mate on his ship and that his illustrated journal was practice for official log-keeping duties he would assume when he became first mate.

Occasionally a sailing journal comes to light that is not only a personal record of a rather uneventful voyage of a whaling ship or merchant vessel, but is a record of one man's fate in the struggle between nations for the supremacy of the sea. Such a journal is that of Seth Barlow, an American aboard the brig *Nancy*, captured on 29 May, 1810, during its voyage "from New York to Gottenbourgh" by the Danish privateer *North Star*. The *Nancy* and her crew were taken to Trondheim, Norway, where there was obviously little else for Seth Barlow to do except write an account of his unintended visit abroad.

Barlow's journal displays his talent for the highly refined Spenserian handwriting of the period as well as an obvious artistic bent. The journal is heavily embellished with ink drawings of ships colored with shades of sepia wash. The text belabors the indignity felt on the part of its author at being held captive illegally and his futile efforts in attempting to secure his freedom. In the manner of a true seaman, this victim of international privateering did not begin one entry, even when not under sail, without recording the weather conditions and wind direction in the first sentence. One such entry, written from Trondheim on Monday, 16 July, reads:

> This day some showers of rane Wind at W.S.W. Wrote two letters
> to send to Rochester the one directed to Cook Brownell and the

Many journal-keepers were adept at drawing, and their ship sketches were accurate in rigging and sail detail. This drawing of the American bark Madonna, *sighted at sea, is from the log of a seaman aboard a nineteenth-century merchant vessel.* FLAYDERMAN COLLECTION

other to Joseph Davis. May Prosperity attend them [the letters] that they arrive and find our friends all well. . . . Employed at home all day. . . . A ship, a schooner and two brigs arrived but have not learnt from whence they came. Got information that they will not give up our protections. But I intend to put myself in a way to obtain them if there is any way to the law. They have no more rite to our protections, than the Devil has to holy warter, took a round turn in the evening. Allen Dexter and Silas Briggs have undertook

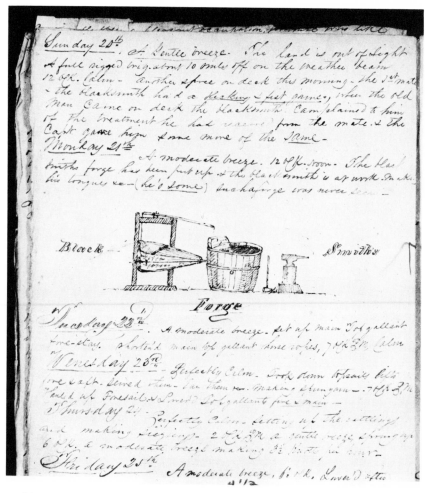

Illustration of a blacksmith's forge built on shipboard.
FLAYDERMAN COLLECTION

to Cypher and the art of Navigation. So ends the day. William Jaction better.

As a means of taking up more time on a day that was obviously as uneventful as most of the others when Seth Barlow remained a prisoner, he decorated this entry with a drawing of what is probably a municipal building in the town in which he was held.

The Barlow journal is important as a historical document and also as the record of one man's anguish at being held captive against his will. It expresses the frustration encountered in an early period of American bureaucracy during a time when communication with other countries was slow and difficult. With the passing of a century and a half, the frustrations and observations of Seth Barlow still seem pertinent.

From the few examples illustrated here of logbooks and journals written by sailing men in the nineteenth century, it should be easy to understand why these are in such demand by collectors and sell for premium prices today. Those that are graphically illustrated or represent important periods in the history of seafaring nations all contribute something to the documentation of the sailing-ship era. The best of the journals, moreover, are examples of folk art.

3
NAUTICAL INSTRUMENTS

Considering the amount of traffic on the oceans and the great fortunes invested in building and outfitting sailing ships prior to the eighteenth century, it is difficult to believe that so many found their way to their destinations and back without the help of the most rudimentary navigational aids. The real beginning of the science of navigation as it is known today is no farther away than the seventeenth century, when the telescope, the pendulum, logarithms, and instruments for measuring minute angles of the sky were all developed or improved upon. Navigational information was passed on from one generation of seafarers to another through the written word and through stories of those who had dared go farther than their own country's coastline. The master of the *Mayflower* was little

Sandglasses, used with a knotted logline for measuring a ship's speed. Glass on the left has a whalebone case. FLAYDERMAN COLLECTION

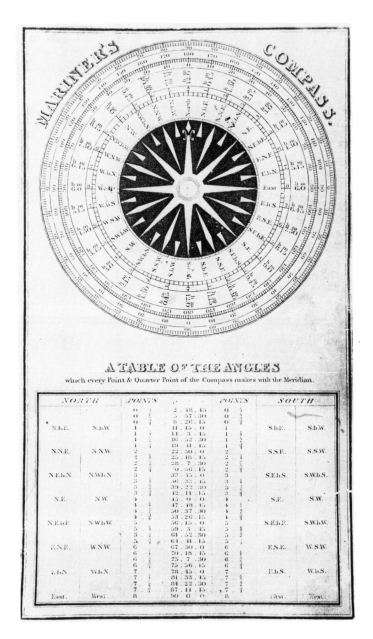

Compass card with table of angles. SUFFOLK COUNTY WHALING MUSEUM

better informed than Christopher Columbus in the use of navigation. Columbus used information he had gained from the Portuguese explorers who had sailed in earlier times.

By the start of the eighteenth century it was usual for ships to

A whaling ship's compass made by Blunt and Nichols, New York. SUFFOLK COUNTY WHALING MUSEUM

Quadrant marked "E. Blow fecit, November 18, 1720." FLAYDERMAN COLLECTION

venture into unknown waters. Their masters trusted to logline, sand-glass and compass, and lacking a chronometer, figured their longitude by "dead reckoning." They kept track of their latitude position by means of a quadrant.

The compass has a longer history as an aid to navigation than any other ship's instrument still in use. There is evidence that Scandinavian sailors used it as early as the thirteenth century. By the fourteenth century the compass seems to have been common in European navigation. The earliest compasses were made with bronze bowls and wooden floats, a lodestone being used as a pointer.

Prince Henry of Portugal—under whose rule voyages were taken that led to the discovery of the Cape Verde Islands in 1447 and of Sierra Leone in 1460—is responsible for collating astronomical information discovered in ancient times and applying this knowledge to the science of navigation. Although man was aware that the altitudes of the sun and stars varied with respect to the location of the observer according to fixed laws, this information was not used by sailors until the fifteenth century to determine latitude and longitude. Seamen relied upon the position of the Pole Star to guide them, but that is as far as celestial navigation had gone.

Next to the compass or magnetic needle, the most important discovery in navigation was an instrument to measure the angular distance of the sun from the celestial equator. Once these angles could be determined, they could be utilized by means of astronomical tables to find a ship's distance north or south of the earth's equator in degrees or fractions thereof.

Prince Henry's son, John II of Portugal, continued his father's work on navigation and employed a "Committee on Navigation" to collect and collate new data and to improve the design of the cross-staff, the instrument then in use for taking observations for latitude at sea. The Committee recommended that the astrolabe be used instead. In Columbus's time a shipmaster had the aid of a cross-staff or

Sea chart made in 1764 showing Louisiana and coast of Florida. FLAYDERMAN COLLECTION

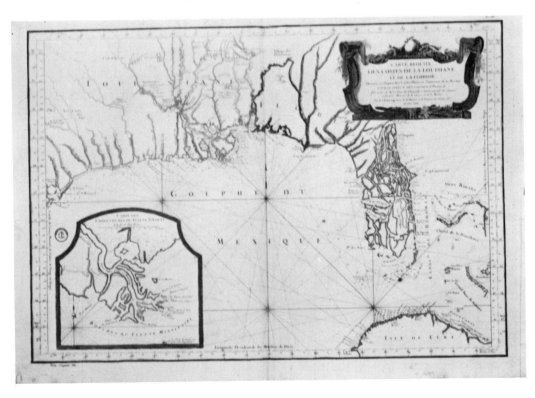

astrolabe, a compass, a table of the sun's declination, a table for connecting the altitude of the Pole Star and, if he was fortunate, some sort of sea chart.

These early charts, although beautifully drawn and painted, were not often very accurate. The first sea chart ever seen in England was carried there in 1489 by Bartholomew Columbus. Through the next two centuries, information was adjusted or added as it became available through navigators and sea captains.

The astrolabe was a more convenient instrument than the primitive cross-staff and is thought to have been invented by the Arabs as early as the tenth century. It was known and used by Portuguese and Spanish seamen in the sixteenth and seventeenth centuries. It was a copper disk suspended from above with a plumb line beneath.

By the eighteenth century both the astrolabe and the cross-staff had been replaced by the more accurate and convenient quadrant. In the nineteenth century the sextant was the instrument used for finding a ship's position by measuring the angles with respect to the sun and the stars.

Solving the problem of how to calculate accurate longitude at sea

Left: Octant inscribed "Made by Ja⁰ Gilbert on Tower Hill for Capᵗ Willᵐ McNeill febʳʸ 20, 1768 London." Right: Octant made for the United States Navy by Spencer-Browning Co., London instrument maker. FLAYDERMAN COLLECTION

 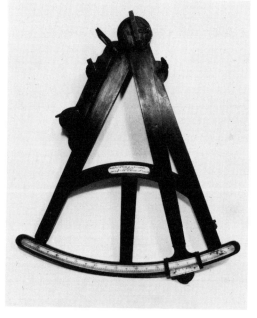

was far more baffling than figuring latitude. Newton was still to provide an answer to that problem when astronomers pondered on a method of longitudinal measurements for navigators. It was not until the invention of the chronometer by John Harrison in the middle of the eighteenth century that longitude could be measured at sea with any real accuracy.

Harrison's discovery culminated a lengthy search for a solution to accurate longitudinal measuring at sea. But his reward was minimal in the face of evidence we have that offers by heads of state in the countries where navigation was important had been piling up for centuries. King Philip of Spain had promised a reward of one thousand crowns to anyone who could discover a safe and accurate method of finding longitude. The States-General of Holland followed with an offer of ten thousand florins. In 1674 England established Greenwich Observatory for the benefit of navigation and especially hoped to calculate the moon's exact position with respect to fixed stars a year in advance. This would provide more accurate tables and a safer guide for sailors.

It sometimes happens that a national disaster leads to the awareness of the necessity for changes or improvements in safety methods. The need for finding a more accurate way to determine navigational positions was brought home to England when Sir Cloudesley Shovel, an esteemed British admiral, was lost with his entire fleet off the Scilly Islands in 1707. The accident was due to a miscalculation in reckoning position.

In 1714 a Royal Commission for the Discovery of Longitude at Sea was appointed and a group of prizes offered for the invention of an accurate chronometer. The prizes varied according to closeness in accuracy, and five thousand pounds was the reward offered for a chronometer that would enable a ship six months from home to find her longitude within sixty miles. If the limit of error was within forty miles the winner would receive seventy-five hundred pounds; and if the position could be calculated to be correct within thirty miles, a prize of ten thousand pounds would be won. A special premium of twenty thousand pounds would be given to the inventor of any method of determining longitude at sea within thirty miles. The bill proclaiming these prizes was enacted by Parliament. In 1716 the Regent of France offered one hundred thousand francs to anyone who could come up with a solution similar to that sought by the British.

Brass and mahogany marine barometer from a nineteenth-century ship, made by D. Primavesi, Cardiff. FLAYDERMAN COLLECTION

John Harrison of Yorkshire was an expert watchmaker and followed this contest with interest. He vowed to devote as many years of his life as necessary to produce the desired accurate chronometer. By 1736, after many trials, Harrison developed a "gridiron pendulum clock" which, on a voyage from Greenwich to Lisbon, proved to be accurate enough to correct the ship's reckoning within several miles. The Royal Commission urged Harrison to concentrate solely on improving his clock and to compete for the prizes. The Commission supplied him with funds, and he spent the next twenty-four years perfecting his chronometer. At the age of sixty-eight Harrison wrote the Commission that he had an instrument he felt qualified for the prizes. The Commission sent Harrison's son, William, on a voyage to Jamaica to test the chronometer's accuracy.

When the ship returned to England after an absence of 147 days, the total variation was found to be less than two minutes, or eighteen miles of longitude. Obviously, Harrison was entitled to the rewards for which he had worked most of his life. But the Commission decided that the clock should be tested once more. A five-month voyage to Barbados proved that the clock showed a variation to Greenwich time of only sixteen seconds. Further tests were still demanded, but it is a matter of record that Harrison did see twenty thousand pounds of the prize money shortly before he died of old age.

The invention of the accurate chronometer by Harrison was second in navigational importance only to the compass. However, it was expensive, and thus did not become standard equipment on most sailing ships until the nineteenth century.

For the collectors of nautical instruments there are still some examples of relatively early objects from which to choose. Barometers, binnacles, calipers, chronometers, compasses, nocturnals, protractors, quadrants or octants and sextants were all used by sailing ships. There are still some examples from the late eighteenth and early nineteenth centuries of many of these beautifully made navigational aids. They were all produced by the countries that engaged in seafaring, and most collectors search for navigational instruments that pertain to a particular sphere of interest in the history of the sea. For instance, there is great interest in the United States in instruments removed from old whaling vessels or from Yankee clipper ships. Instruments in wooden cases are also searched for—and when the cases have been painted or otherwise decorated by hand, this is a bonus for any collector. A brass binnacle with attached lamps can be an attrac-

Left: A ship's brass engine-room telegraph converted into a handsome floor lamp. FLAYDERMAN COLLECTION *Right: Brass ship's binnacle with oil lamps attached.* FLAYDERMAN COLLECTION

tive addition to any collection, but a rather special find is the carved and inlaid Victorian binnacle illustrated here. Loglines, used to measure a ship's speed through the water are extremely difficult to find today, but the sandglasses used in conjunction with them sometimes become available.

Elaborate ship's binnacle with nautical motifs in wood inlay around the sides. Inscribed "Wm. Harris Co., Holborn, London." FLAYDER-MAN COLLECTION

Collecting navigational instruments is a rather special field within the area of nautical antiques, but in studying them it is obvious that their makers realized that a great deal depended upon the accuracy of their manufacture. The safety of a crew and its ship was in the hands of the instrument maker.

4

SEA CHARTS AND SAILORS' HANDBOOKS

If the early seafarer did not have the most sophisticated navigational aids to guide him on his journeys, there was other knowledge available that was somewhat dependable and helpful. An understanding of the wind and the weather and the variables of the world's oceans went side by side with the art of seafaring. The Portuguese, for instance, observed that the winds that began as northerlies down their coastline in the summer could propel their ships at least to the nearer Atlantic Islands. These winds became known as trade winds because of their value to the merchant sailing ships of the world. Ancient voyages of Indian, Arab, Chinese and Polynesian sailors were guided by a similar observation of trade winds in their part of the world. They understood the vagaries of the alternating monsoons of the Indian Ocean. This type of knowledge was recorded on ancient maps and charts.

All sailors eventually learned to take advantage not only of wind currents but also of ocean currents. They realized that the most advantageous routes to sail were not direct distances between two points. Rather, they chose routes where wind and ocean currents would move their ships swiftly. By the time Vasco da Gama made his voyage from Portugal around South Africa to India in 1497, thus opening a sea route for trade and colonial expansion between Europe and the Far East, he had had the experience of fifty years of navigation as a guide. Columbus's voyage pointed out the existence of the best sailing routes to the West Indies, and ships that followed

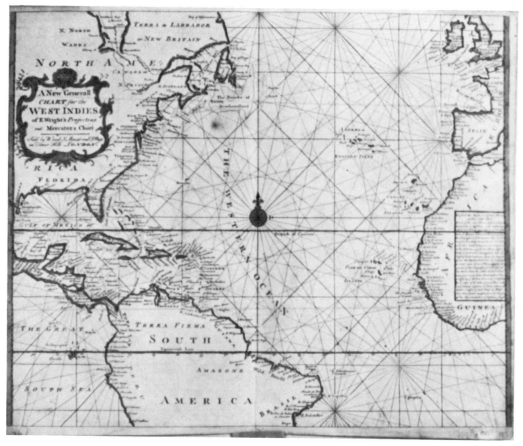

Chart made in 1759 showing the West Indies. FLAYDERMAN
COLLECTION

his route discovered the Gulf Stream that ran northward along the Atlantic coastline of America.

While the art of making sea charts and maps began with the Mediterranean countries in the West, ancient Oriental charts of a more primitive nature have been found made of seashells sewn to reeds with palm fiber. Early navigators were eager to record their knowledge of the mysterious sea for future voyages.

There was always a great amount of superstition surrounding the oceans. The existing early sea charts, or portulans, painted on parchment or vellum by the Mediterranean artists, exhibit examples of sea monsters, strange-looking natives and little vignettes of men being devoured by monster lobsters and ships being choked by mammoth sea serpents. On some of the early charts the buildings of important cities along a coastline have been drawn in along with their heraldic banners for identification. These sixteenth-century hand-painted charts might have offered some aid to the mariner, but they were considered to be more works of art that appealed to the merchant shipowners than aids to navigation. Of interest to modern collectors is the similarity in style of the tiny paintings of figures and buildings on these charts to many of the illustrations in later sea logs and journals.

More practical charts, although less artistic, became available after the invention of copperplate engraving in the middle of the sixteenth century, but new findings were added slowly. The rise of Dutch seapower was marked by the publication of an atlas, *The Mariner's Mirror*, which appeared in 1584. This was translated into English and included elevations of the coastlines. The Dutch soon became the major producers of maps, sea charts and atlases, which were translated and published by all countries involved in sea trade. The maps could be purchased as practical printed devices, and they could be embellished by painters who specialized in this type of work. Many of the unpainted maps of this period were painted at a later date to be more appealing to collectors.

The first English sea atlas was published by John Seller in 1671 from old Dutch plates. Shortly afterward Captain Grenville Collins was appointed to survey and measure all the seacoasts of the kingdom and to take bearings of the headlands. The result of this survey was the publication in 1693 of *Great Britain's Coasting Pilot*, which continued in publication for one hundred years.

The seventeenth- and eighteenth-century charts gradually became less ornate artistically and more accurate scientifically as cartographers such as J. F. W. DesBarres, Captain James Cook and Captain Thomas Hurd charted the North American coastline. Captain Cook held the artistic charts in disdain and pleaded for use of the sea chart as a purely navigational instrument. After the establishment of the Hydrographic Department of the Admiralty in 1795, Cook's theory of the value of unornamented, functional sea charts was adhered to. While less artistic than the earlier charts, these are the ones that are most available for today's collector.

Many navigational instruments were useless without the proper mathematical and celestial charts and tables that went with them. Compass cards with tables of angles, books of sailing directions and

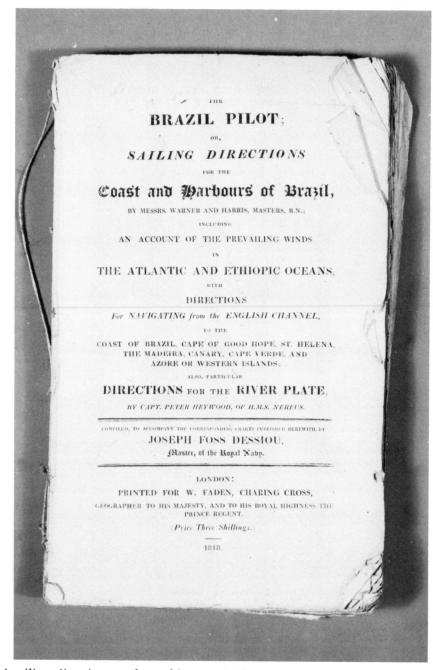

THE

BRAZIL PILOT;

OR,

SAILING DIRECTIONS

FOR THE

Coast and Harbours of Brazil,

BY MESSRS. WARNER AND HARRIS, MASTERS, R.N.;

INCLUDING

AN ACCOUNT OF THE PREVAILING WINDS

IN

THE ATLANTIC AND ETHIOPIC OCEANS,

WITH

DIRECTIONS

For NAVIGATING from the ENGLISH CHANNEL,

TO THE

COAST OF BRAZIL, CAPE OF GOOD HOPE, ST. HELENA,
THE MADEIRA, CANARY, CAPE VERDE, AND
AZORE OR WESTERN ISLANDS;

ALSO, PARTICULAR

DIRECTIONS FOR THE **RIVER PLATE**,

BY CAPT. PETER HEYWOOD, OF H.M.S. NEREUS.

COMPILED, TO ACCOMPANY THE CORRESPONDING CHARTS PUBLISHED HEREWITH, BY

JOSEPH FOSS DESSIOU,

Master, of the Royal Navy.

LONDON:

PRINTED FOR W. FADEN, CHARING CROSS,

GEOGRAPHER TO HIS MAJESTY, AND TO HIS ROYAL HIGHNESS THE
PRINCE REGENT.

(Price Three Shillings.)

1818.

Handbooks and sailing directions such as this were indispensable to navigators. FLAYDERMAN COLLECTION

navigational handbooks were published. All of this information—some more accurate than others—was used throughout the eighteenth and nineteenth centuries.

Nevil Maskeleyne, Astronomer Royal, published the *British Nautical Almanac* in 1767. Early copies of this standard work are collectors' items today. Early editions of Nathaniel Bowditch's *The Practical Navigator* are always in demand, as is the handbook of navigation from which it was derived, written by the Englishman John Hamilton Morse.

Nathaniel Bowditch, of Salem, Massachusetts was responsible for eliminating many costly errors from navigational literature of the early nineteenth century. His handbook, although based on Morse's earlier work, became standard equipment for seamen for generations after its first publication in 1802. Bowditch, a mathematical genius, found no less than eight thousand errors in Morse's work, and when he published what had started out to be a revision, he did so under his own name.

There are, of course, many other navigational handbooks of the late eighteenth and early nineteenth centuries. Many of these were incorrect and incomplete, and no one was more aware of this than the sea captains and navigators who wrote them. It would be many years before maps, charts and current information would be collated for safer sea travel. However, to the marine historian, this early printed information is of great interest.

5

FIGUREHEADS
AND OTHER CARVED
SHIP ORNAMENTS

Nowhere was the mysticism surrounding ships and life on the sea better expressed by the craftsmen involved in shipbuilding and decoration than in the fascinating figure carvings that adorned the bows of sailing ships. The use of the figurehead goes far back in maritime history. The Romans used a swan as bow decoration, and the symbol of the Phoenician trading vessel was the horse. During the sixteenth century, ships were decorated with bronze animal figures and small shield devices. These decorations evolved into beaks and thence to animal shapes, with the lion's head becoming a popular subject.

As international trade developed, the ships of various nations were built with figure carvings that represented their country of origin. It is interesting that in the beginning of the eighteenth century the ships that traded in the Orient began to exhibit carvings of Chinese figures. These probably appeared less menacing to the people into whose ports these foreign ships appeared with great frequency.

There is small value to the collector in discussing the history of ships' carvings in detail here. During the baroque period there was little space on a ship's exterior that did not exhibit some form of the woodcarver's art. However, very little exists today that can be traced to that period of lavish ship decoration, and even carvings from later centuries are scarce. The bulk of the remaining examples are in museums.

The woodcarvings that do exist today are mainly in the form of figureheads or bow ornamentation, stern carvings, and mast- and rudder-decorated wood. Of all of these, the figurehead is the most desirable as a collector's item—and certainly the most difficult to find. Figureheads that do exist are mainly from the nineteenth century, although museums in the maritime nations of the world have examples from an earlier period. These earlier works of wood sculpture show the art at its best. They represent a broad area of subjects, for as the lion's head gave way to other forms for bow decoration, the carver's and the shipbuilder's imaginations were allowed to dictate ingenious designs. These might represent the ship's purpose as a trader, whaling vessel or naval ship. One sometimes wonders whether

Left:Figurehead from the four-masted bark Falkland *of Liverpool, launched in 1889 and wrecked off the Scilly Isles in June 1901 with the loss of her captain and five of his crew. Right: Figurehead from the Italian bark* Lofaro, *wrecked on the Merrick Rock, Isles of Scilly, on February 2, 1902. Ship and crew were lost, but the buxom carving survived.* BOTH PHOTOS: VALHALLA MARITIME MUSEUM

Left: Figurehead from unknown ship, circa 1830. SHEL-
BURNE MUSEUM *Right: Figurehead of "Liberty" carved in
the quarter-round.* SHELBURNE MUSEUM

the name of a ship or the figurehead came first on vessels with figureheads that were so appropriate for their names. What is known is
that by the period of transoceanic sailing ships, almost every nation
that owned vessels had ships adorned with and identified by their
figureheads.

As in most areas of the decorative arts in America, the shipbuilders
fashioned their earliest efforts after the British prototypes with which
they were familiar. Eventually, American shipbuilders began to excel
in their trade and their ships took on lines indigenous only to American-built vessels. The figureheads made for those ships took on a
national character, too.

Since figurehead carving was not considered a major art, few records were ever kept as to the makers of these folk carvings. In many
cases the figureheads in American museums record histories of the
ships they once adorned. But the men who designed, carved and
painted the figureheads are lost in the anonymity of most folk artists

of the eighteenth and nineteenth centuries.

By the nineteenth century every important seaport in America and Europe had its master carvers who supplied figures and other carved wood pieces for the many ships built during the height of the sailing-ship era. The same seaport woodcarvers were also adept at making furniture, trade signs, weather vanes and other wooden objects. In America, the figurehead carver also did a respectable business carving cigar-store Indians and other three-dimensional trade figures.

The use of the figurehead throughout sailing history is probably at least in part due to the widespread illiteracy among seafarers. A figurehead identified its ship just as a figural trade sign was an aid to a prospective shopper who could not read. Ships were identified by their figureheads in all the ports of the world.

Although there are few collectors today who can afford the occasional figurehead that comes up for sale, magnificent examples of

Left: Figurehead from the brig Sea Nymph, *built around 1800 in Duxbury, Massachusetts, for the West Indies trade.* SHELBURNE MUSEUM *Right:. Figurehead from the whaling ship* Jefferson. SUFFOLK COUNTY WHALING MUSEUM

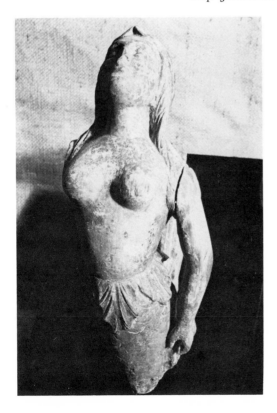 

figureheads can be seen in scattered museums throughout the world. The carved ship figurehead is one of the most romantic and fascinating relics of the sailing-ship era. But smaller carvings from other parts of ships offer a variety of subjects for collectors, and these are sometimes more readily available. Fortunately, both Britain and America have excellent museum collections of figureheads and ship carvings that can be studied and enjoyed. The figureheads of any country's ships are original folk art. Each has its own personality, but somehow tells us less about the man who carved it than the ship it adorned.

The subjects used for figureheads in the eighteenth and nineteenth centuries are as varied as the names of the ships that carried them. Many reflect their ship's part in helping to mold naval history. One figurehead, a golden lion couchant, is in the superb collection of the Museum of the Marine Historical Association in Mystic, Connecticut. This lion figurehead was removed from the H.M. Brig *Boxer*, which was captured by the U.S. Brig *Enterprise* on 6 September, 1813, in a fierce battle off the Maine coast. Since both ships were badly damaged in this famous sea battle, it is not known when the figurehead was removed. The captains of both ships died of their wounds.

Human figures were the most prevalent subjects used as prow decoration. Partially draped or fully clothed women's figures were popular. For sailors during months on the sea, this was the only female companionship they had. Busts and full figures of men ranged from national heroes, figures in mythology and well-known members of the nobility to sculptures of the shipowner or a member of his family. The symbol of the British lion was used on the earliest American ships, but it gave way to the figure of the carved eagle during the first spurt of American nationalism at the end of the eighteenth century. Rather unpleasant-looking gargoyles also led their ships across the ocean, as did playful dolphins or cherubic carvings of Aeolus, mythological father of the winds.

Many of the existing figureheads are of unknown origin, their history having faded into oblivion along with the ships they once led across the world's oceans. Perhaps the most diversified collection of figureheads in the world exists in Tresco, the Isles of Scilly. This group of one hundred and forty-five small islands and reefs lying twenty-eight miles southwest of Land's End, in Cornwall, were at one time occupied by pirates and smugglers. Because of unusual climatic conditions and the fact that the area is extremely rocky, there have been an inordinate number of shipwrecks through the centuries of ocean travel in that area. A collection of figureheads and carved ornaments salvaged from foundered ships is housed in a museum aptly named Valhalla, after the mythological hall of immortality into which the heroes slain in battle are received.

The Valhalla Maritime Museum was founded about 1840 by Augustus Smith, Lord Proprietor of the Isles, and the collection now comprises relics salvaged from over one thousand ships. One is also reminded of the efforts on the part of some of the inhabitants of the Scillys who braved many storms in order to save the lives of ship-wrecked crews.

While many of the carvings and other relics at Tresco are of ships of unknown origin, others recall stories of gallant rescues and perilous adventures on dark nights in turbulent seas. One figurehead, from the 600-ton Spanish bark *Primros*, helped to save the life of the only survivor out of a crew of twelve when the ship, bound for

Figurehead depicting an unknown man. FLAYDERMAN COLLECTION

45

Falmouth from Havana with a cargo of sugar, struck a rock formation known as The Seven Stones at 5 A.M. on 24 June 1871 and sank in twelve minutes. The one survivor, a seaman named Vincenzo Defelice, kept himself afloat for several hours by clutching the ship's figurehead, a life-sized female figure, until he was able to sight one of the ship's lifeboats and row ashore.

There are many other Scilly figureheads from ships that struck uncharted rock and went down, although in many cases all the crew were saved. In some instances "the vessel was a total wreck, but the crew and ship's stores were saved." Many of these wrecks provided the islanders with stores of generous proportions. A 662-ton tea clipper, the *Friar Tuck*, was driven onto Newfort Island on 2 December, 1863, in one of the worst gales ever known to the British Isles. The cargo of tea the ship was carrying to London from China was "acquired" by the islanders. The bow decoration from the

Female figurehead attached to the original ship's beam.
SHELBURNE MUSEUM

46

The Friar Tuck *was a tea clipper launched in Aberdeen, Scotland. In 1857, bound for London from China, she was driven by gales into St. Mary's Harbour, Scilly Islands, and wrecked on December 27.* VALHALLA MARITIME MUSEUM

Palinurus, a ship lost on Lion Rock on 27 December, 1848, represents another "gift from the sea" for the islanders. All hands were lost in the wreck, and the islanders recovered and buried seventeen bodies. Washed up along with the bodies were seventy-one puncheons and fourteen hogsheads of spirits, together with nine casks of rum.

The figureheads displayed at Valhalla Maritime Museum are a superb representation of the variety of subjects used as bow carvings in the late eighteenth century and throughout the nineteenth. The notoriously vicious waters surrounding the Isles were not at all selective in their victims; Italian, Spanish, Portuguese, French, Dutch, Norwegian, Austrian, Danish, American and British ships are all represented in the collection. One has only to look at the records of the demise of ships from every seafaring nation to realize how many ships foundered off the Isles of Scilly during the sailing-ship days.

The figureheads and other ship carvings that comprise the Valhalla Maritime Museum collection have all been expertly restored to their original state with the exception of one, which has been left in

Oculus carving, or "ship's eye," which has been used as a prow decoration for centuries by superstitious seamen. (Early 1800s.) SHEL-BURNE MUSEUM

its original weathered condition for comparison. The restored figure-heads are all mounted at the angle at which they originally appeared on the bows of their ships. One can observe the forward movement given to these figures by their carvers, and the viewer can also com-pare figureheads used on ships of various countries. This group of figureheads points out that ship carving was an international art.

Although earlier ships were decorated from stem to stern with carved, gilded and painted ornaments, today's collector can find only the carvings from eighteenth- and nineteenth-century ships. These are limited to figureheads, stern carvings, rudder ornaments, mast boards and gangway boards. Occasionally a carved coat-of-arms, escutcheon, or an American eagle is offered for sale, but these have become more and more scarce in recent years.

One of the most ancient forms of external ship decoration is the oculus, sometimes called "ship's eye," which has been used on vessels of many types from ancient times to the present. The origins of this symbol are somewhat vague, but it is thought to be the eye of Horus, the Egyptian hawk-headed god of day. The eye, carved or painted on the prow of a ship, was probably meant to be a superstitious "aid to navigation" in the times when there were no other ways of calculating a ship's position.

The figurehead probably had its origins in the ancient tradition of draping an animal skin over the prow of a ship. This was a symbolic sacrificial offering to the gods, and by the sixteenth century carvings were used on many external parts of the ship.

The men who sailed ships across oceans to unknown continents were not especially known for their traditional religious fervor, but they developed a religion of their own based on superstition and legend. The dangerous, risky nature of their work led them to depend upon any external symbol that might be good luck for their ships. Certain figureheads and their ships became known for bringing bad luck or for being out of favor with whatever gods governed life on the sea. Even in today's enlightened world, there are fishermen who do not tempt fate: on their boats they carry rams' horns or other sacrificial instruments. The oculus can still be found painted on fishing boat prows in some ports of Portugal and Sicily.

Stern carvings were used in profusion during the seventeenth century. They represented the owners of the ships, or were simply a

Detail, American Indian *stern carving.* SHELBURNE MUSEUM

American stern carving: Indian in center with tobacco leaf and books, surrounded by globe and charts. From the ship American Indian *of North River, Plymouth County, Massachusetts, circa 1785.* SHELBURNE MUSEUM

variety of architectural motifs from the baroque period of decoration. Cherubs, cupids, coats of arms, figures of an allegorical nature, dolphins, masks, garlands and animals were used. By the middle of the seventeenth century, ship ornamentation had reached its height, and there were few external parts of a large ship that did not have some elaborate ornamental carving. These lavish decorations did not add to the function of a ship in any way, and in the case of warships they were a deterrent to fast maneuverability because of the extra weight. Ornamentation, especially on warships, declined in amount during the eighteenth century, and the heavy figures were dispensed with in favor of lighter surface decoration of a more conservative nature.

Stern boards, name boards and stern carvings of the nineteenth century can be seen in maritime museums, and some are also in private collections. The stern carving illustrated here is a particularly graceful carving of a sailor and his lady, and is the traditional "Sailor's Farewell." Stern carvings on American ships were often friezes of a patriotic nature. A carving of this type in the Shelburne

Carved dragonhead rudder ornament, eighteenth century.
FLAYDERMAN COLLECTION

Carved rudder ornaments. FLAYDERMAN COLLECTION

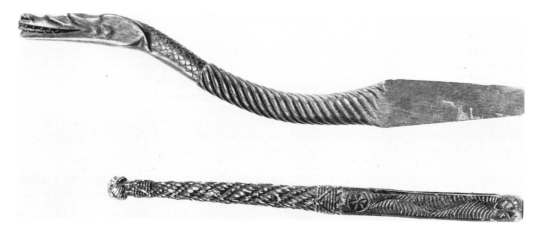

Left: Carved rudderhead, early nineteenth century. FLAY-
DERMAN COLLECTION *Right: Carved rudderhead, eighteenth
century.* FLAYDERMAN COLLECTION

Museum collection is nine feet long and represents an American
Indian with a tobacco leaf. It was taken from the ship *American
Indian*, of Plymouth County, Massachusetts, and dates from the late
eighteenth century.

Carved or patterned rudders were frequently figures of serpents,
dragons or demons, subjects dictated by the elongated shape of the
rudder. Those that can be found today are mostly from inland water-
way boats such as Venetian galleys or barges and Dutch canal boats.
The Dutch delighted in ornamenting their boats with carved work,
as did owners of many small boats all over the world. To discuss
thoroughly ship or boat decoration in respect to its worldwide representation would be an impossibility within an entire volume, let
alone one chapter. All that can be done is to give the collector some
idea of the examples of decorative carvings that might still be found.

Rudderheads, such as those illustrated here, are in great demand
by collectors both for their value as maritime relics and as decorative
examples of the woodcarver's art. Carved boards from boarding lad-

Left: Carved board from mast, showing sailor leaning on capstan. FLAYDERMAN COLLECTION *Right: Carved mast board with foul anchor.* FLAYDERMAN COLLECTION

ders and mast boards are sought for the same reasons. Because of the inability of wood to stand up for many years after it has been exposed to salt water, wind and rain, only a minute percentage of the carved figures that once decorated ships has survived. These fragments that do still exist all contribute something to the scant knowledge we have of the vast subject of ship decoration.

Gangway board with eagle carving. FLAYDERMAN COLLECTION

Left: Carved gunport covers with anchors. FLAYDERMAN COLLECTION

6
RELICS OF THE CHINA TRADE DAYS

When the Portuguese seafarers first traded with China at the beginning of the sixteenth century, they discovered a peaceful and highly civilized nation. As more and more Western merchant ships found their way to the other side of the world in search of a variety of lucrative merchandise, the Chinese became aware that all nations did not come in peace and friendship. Therefore, they set up rules and regulations so that there would be as little contact as possible between them and the "Western barbarians." Between 1514 and the end of the eighteenth century, China found itself surrounded by ships and land traders, and the history of East and West during those years is rampant with examples of mistrust and misunderstanding.

In 1634 China set up strict regulations to govern trade with the West, an action that they felt necessary when the Dutch traders came. Great Britain, which had established the East India Company, was content with the products they could take out of India and did not turn to China until the eighteenth century. By that time Chinese trade was limited to the town of Canton, which was the principal area for commerce and, after 1757, became the only town where dealing with foreigners was allowed.

The Chinese merchants set up small representative groups called co-hongs, and all trade was handled through them. The co-hongs and the hongs, which housed the foreigners, were situated well outside the city of Canton, and further travel inland was forbidden to outsiders. This was to avoid contact as far as possible with the Chinese

Hongs on Canton River with foreign ships (at right foreground) and Chinese junks. Flags of trading countries fly over the warehouses and living compounds. The settlement was wiped out during the Opium War with England.
FLAYDERMAN COLLECTION

people. A further precaution was taken by forbidding the Chinese language to be taught to foreigners. Trading was conducted in a pidgin, or business, English, which was really a mixture of Chinese, English, Dutch and Portuguese.

By the time American ships arrived, following the Revolution, the regulated system of trade with China was well established. Trading was honorable, peaceful and extremely profitable for all parties. The Chinese merchants involved became rich and powerful, and the fortunes of the shipowners from the trading companies of the West increased accordingly. However, it rankled many of the Western shipowners that there was less selling than buying in their dealings with the Chinese. There was little that the highly developed nation of China needed or wanted from distant lands, so it demanded gold and silver for its goods.

Sea captains could have portraits painted by Chinese artists while their ships were at Canton. Oriental features were usually given to Westerners in these portraits. FLAYDER-MAN COLLECTION

Finding a commodity for which Chinese goods could be bartered became a constant problem for the Western traders. Ginseng root, which grew in New England and New York, was believed by the Chinese to give them immortality. The *Empress of China*, the first American vessel to trade independently with the Chinese, brought thirty tons of the root to barter. Otter skins were a prized fur in China, and American shipowners purchased these from the Indians on the northwest coast of America and sought sealskins in the Antarctic and the South Seas. Sandalwood, edible birds' nests, sea cucumbers and sharks' fins were also acceptable goods in China, and ships arrived at Canton loaded with these. However, the almost insatiable demand in the West for Chinese silks, tea, porcelain and other goods

56

forced Western merchants to leave a great deal of hard cash in the hands of the Chinese.

The East India Company and the American traders were aware that there was one illegal commodity that would find a ready market in China and earn enormous profits for them. The British, with easy access to the opium fields of India, carried great quantities of the forbidden drug to the illegal market in China. This trade required fast ships and hard-driving captains. The vessels were fashioned after the Baltimore clippers that had served as privateers during the American Revolution and as pirate ships and slave ships in the early part of the nineteenth century.

American traders had to find their opium in a different part of the world from the British. They imported their shipments of the drug from Turkey and also acted as agents for the British in selling Indian opium. Profits were enormous, and it is probable that almost every shipping company involved in trade with the Orient engaged in drug traffic to some extent. The more voyages a company could get out of a ship, the better. Moreover, since the cargoes were so valuable and trading was done surreptitiously along the China coast, there was a danger of being pursued and overtaken, not only by the Chinese but by pirates. It was obvious that a swift ship would have a great advantage.

By 1839 China had a drug problem so serious that the Emperor sent an envoy to Canton, who forced the British to turn over a fortune in opium to the Chinese government. This action led to the Opium War, which ended with England owning the island of Hong Kong, from which they could continue their drug traffic without interruption. Nor was the United States without its spoils. In 1844 they negotiated a treaty with the Chinese that gave them access to more Chinese ports and a greater opportunity to smuggle the illicit drug into China.

The great profits derived from Chinese trade led to the need for still faster ships. Money was no object in designing and building sleek craft that could outrun all others and turn profits more quickly. Speed records were carefully watched, and the means by which the masters drove their crews to save hours or days in a voyage did not matter. Accusations of cruelty made by a ship's crew were constantly overlooked. There was always a way to man a ship, and, once afloat, a master had methods of dealing with reluctant or lazy seamen.

There was another reason that it became necessary to make faster runs to and from the Orient. By the 1830s most of the cargo to the West was tea. The British and Americans, by this time, had become as addicted to this leaf as the Chinese had to opium. Of the two, tea was more perishable. In addition, the ships that made it back to home port with the first crops of new tea brought the highest profits to their owners. New ship designs were needed. All vessels had to wait for the monsoons and the only advantage one would have over another was to be able to save time on the run home.

The first of the China clippers was designed by an American, Captain Nat Palmer, who convinced shipowner William Low during a voyage from China that a properly designed ship could leave port any time regardless of the monsoon winds. Palmer designed a model of a sleek, sharp-bowed ship, and the Lows had it built. The *Houqua*, launched in the spring of 1844 and named for the co-hong merchant with whom the American traders had enjoyed a profitable and pleasant relationship, was the first American clipper ship. It was by no means a revolutionary design, but rather a refinement of known principles. The sharp hull was made for speed rather than cargo space, and the ship was heavily sparred: more sail meant more speed. To keep this type of ship moving at its full potential, the captain had to become one with the ship. He had to be daredevil and dictator to get as much as possible out of every inch of sail.

A second clipper, the *Rainbow*, was built by Howland and Aspinwall and launched in 1845. This ship cut the run from China to New York from an average of one hundred days to seventy-nine days on her second attempt. The same firm ordered another clipper to be specially built for Captain Robert Waterman, a master who had a reputation among seamen as a demon, but who was revered by shipowners who reaped greater profits from the speed he had been able to get out of his commands.

The ship built for Captain Waterman was the *Sea Witch*, perhaps the most famous of all China clippers. Under the hard-driving Waterman she set the all-time record for the China run. In March 1849 the *Sea Witch* cut the time of the run to seventy-four days and fourteen hours, a record that was never broken. China trade merchants began to order ships with the "sharp look," and the clipper ship fleet grew larger and more profitable.

For today's collector, there are any number of relics of the China trade. However, those interested only in marine antiques search for more specialized objects than the porcelain, silks, lacquer work and other objects that were brought to the West. Material directly related to ships, the port of Canton and the hongs is of special interest for collectors of marine antiques.

Porcelains were painted to order with pictures of a sea captain's vessel as it waited in the harbor for crops to ripen and for favorable winds. A commanding officer could have his portrait painted with a miniature view of his ship in the background, and if he was seen by the artist to have slightly Oriental features, this was how all Occidentals were viewed by the Chinese artists. A favorite scene that was painted on porcelain was a view from the Canton harbor of the hongs with the flags of all trading nations flying in the wind.

Also of special interest are paintings and prints of the activities of the hongs. Views of the busy warehouses, factories and trading between East and West, such as the painting shown here, are rare and of great historical interest. Journals and logs of the China trade days reveal little of the infamous opium traffic, but descriptions of the voyages tell us a lot about the necessity for speed at any price.

7
CLIPPER SHIPS AND SAILING CARDS

Although the fast clipper ships were first developed for the China trade, it was another kind of lucrative cargo that was to spur the building of more and more extreme clippers. When gold was discovered in 1848 at Sutter's Mill, California, it took months before word reached the eastern part of the United States. The news caused a mass exodus, and every available ship was pressed into service for the hazardous voyage around Cape Horn.

Although the transportation of human cargo was nothing new to the American shipping industry, which had been involved in the slave trade for many years, the transportation of thousands of gold seekers was another matter. Again, time was of the essence. Not only were people clamoring for space on the fastest ships in order to be first to stake their claims for the great riches that were promised them, but supplies were needed for the thousands of prospectors from the Midwest who had taken the arduous overland route in the treasure hunt.

Speed meant enormous profits for the shipowners. While there was certainly gold to be found in California, at the beginning it turned out to be almost worthless since there was little or nothing the successful prospector could purchase with it. The ships that could arrive first with food, whiskey, supplies for prospecting and a few luxury goods stood to make the largest profits.

Although the earliest clippers, those designed for the China trade, were the products of New York shipyards, the builders of New Eng-

Right: One share in the missionary ship, Morning Star. *Selling shares was a way of raising money to send missionaries to Pacific islands.* FLAYDERMAN COLLECTION

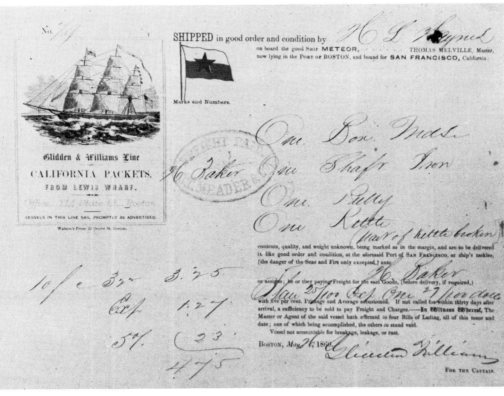

Above: Shipping invoice for a California packet. FLAYDER-
MAN COLLECTION

Booklet containing the story of the Morning Star, *published to tell investors what they would get for their money.* FLAY-DERMAN COLLECTION

MERCHANTS' EXPRESS LINE OF CLIPPER SHIPS FOR SAN FRANCISCO.
Passages 106 & 117 Days.

THE WELL-KNOWN   EXTREME CLIPPER SHIP

EAGLE WING

LINNELL, Commander, is now loading at Pier 10 E. R.
For freight apply at office of   RANDOLPH M. COOLEY, 88 Wall St., Tontine Building.
Agents in San Francisco, Messrs. DE WITT, KITTLE & CO.

American clipper-ship sailing cards advertising a fast passage to San Francisco. Cards were handed out at seaports to attract passengers and shippers. FLAYDERMAN COLLECTION

STRICTLY A 1 EXTREME CLIPPER SHIP.

Coleman's California Line for
SAN FRANCISCO.
THE
GEORGE PEABODY

J. D. PAINE, Commander.
Comes to her berth, PIER 14, EAST RIVER,
with one-third of her Cargo on board, and will have Immediate Dispatch.

This splendid Clipper having Three Decks, makes her the most desirable vessel loading. Being a Fast Sailer, Shippers can depend upon an early delivery of their shipments. For balance of Freight, apply to

WM. T. COLEMAN & CO., 161 Pearl St., near Wall,
Agents in San Francisco, Messrs. WM. T. COLEMAN & CO.

land also rushed to fill orders from speculators and merchants for more and faster ships. Clippers slid down the ways with great frequency, and bonuses were offered to the captains who could make the run around the Horn in less than one hundred days. The swiftest recorded run was made by the *Flying Cloud*, which reached the port of San Francisco in eighty-nine days and twenty-one hours.

It is difficult today to conceive the enormous amounts of money that were to be made by shaving days or even hours from the clipper runs to California. Although relatively few of the gold prospectors were raking in fortunes, the shipping merchants of the East became the real winners in the race for gold. Anyone with money to invest wanted a ship of his own—or at least a share in one—and by 1853 the demand for more and more ships reached a peak. In that year one hundred and twenty-five clippers were launched in American shipyards. Competition almost immediately became too strong and rates dropped rapidly. It appeared that too many ships were sailing and that there was suddenly not enough need for their services. It would be a while, however, before it became obvious that the clipper had been overproduced.

Passage to San Francisco at the height of the gold rush was not cheap, as can be proved by the ticket issued to one Francis D. Law-

Ticket for voyage from Boston to San Francisco at the beginning of gold rush in that city. FLAYDERMAN COLLECTION

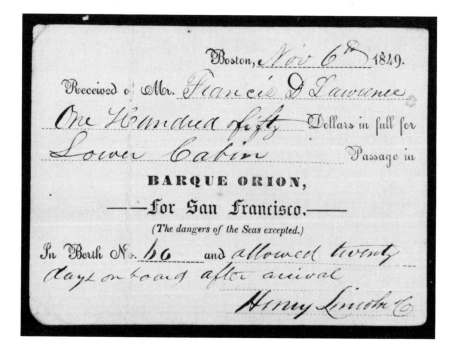

64

Announcement for ships sailing from Bremen and Hamburg, calling at ports in North America, South America or Australia. Bremen and Hamburg were both busy ports for emigrants from Europe. FLAYDERMAN COLLECTION

rence illustrated here. "One hundred fifty dollars" investment for a journey in a lower cabin was a high price in 1849. It is estimated that of the eighty thousand gold seekers who arrived in California that year, half arrived by ship. Since it was not unusual for a ship to make back its cost in a single voyage at the height of the gold rush, it is little wonder that the ships were produced in such numbers. The "twenty days on board after arrival" promised to the ticket holder was no gamble on the part of the shipowners. The passion for gold was so strong that passengers, and often the entire ship's crew, immediately abandoned a vessel in San Francisco harbor. It is estimated that by July 1850 there were five hundred deserted ships in the harbor that were destined never to make a return voyage. However, the fast ships with good captains and loyal crews made run after run with prospectors and supplies.

The discovery of gold in California was followed in 1851 by a gold rush to Australia. While steamers had taken over some of the trading business from sailing ships for the California run, sailing vessels were still very much needed for the longer voyage to Australia. The new British-owned Black Ball Line belonging to James Baines was comprised of packet ships built in Canada from designs similar to those for the American extreme clippers. However, these ships were not able to make the records for speed possible with American-built clippers, and Baines chartered American ships and ordered more to be built. Baines' competitors also bought American ships, and these were as instrumental in the settlement of Australia as their earlier prototypes had been in changing San Francisco from a wilderness to a boom town.

It is difficult to imagine that all this frenzied shipbuilding activity took place within the span of a few years, but by 1854 there were already too many ships and not enough charters. While some vessels were still being built, it was obvious that the great boom had peaked. In 1855 thirty-five new ships were constructed, but these were smaller and lacked the grandeur of the American extreme clippers. There was some financial relief that year for the shipowners, as California was now sending wheat from its port. This gave to the shipowner a profitable return cargo that he had not previously enjoyed.

One problem that faced the owners and captains during the two gold rushes was that of manning the ships. Even though high character was less of a qualification than an able body, many despotic captains had developed reputations that precluded any but the most desperate seamen from signing on with them. Less than honorable means were employed in gathering a crew, and there is good reason, besides the lure of gold, that many sailors helped settle the State of California and the continent of Australia.

The handsome extreme clipper ship of the gold-rush era had a short life. Because of its limited capacity, it was only practical when the profits to be made on passengers and cargo were so great that speed was the most important factor. The smaller, slower ships, although less "sharp" in appearance, were more practical and were designed to carry more cargo at less expense. Although 1855 had been a profitable year for American sea traders, this was due in part to the involvement of British and French ships in the Crimean War. By this time, also, the British were building their own sailing ships for their important tea trade.

Many American clippers ended their days as transporters of Chinese coolies and guano. The coolies were brought to Peru to gather and load the putrid guano, and for most of them, the work meant certain death. Under conditions more terrible than existed on the African slave ships, the kidnapped Chinese were forced into despicable work. As many as a quarter of them died aboard ship; the rest either committed suicide or died from inhaling the terrible odor of the bird droppings they were forced to gather. Coolies were also shipped to the Chinchas (South America), Australia and Cuba. Although this sort of cargo was not relished by the captains of clipper ships, it was highly profitable.

The last American extreme clipper ship to be built was prophetically named the *Twilight,* and it was completed in 1857. This was a year of financial panic, and charters of any sort were difficult to come by. Clipper ships were cut down and pressed into domestic service or laid up in hopes of better days. These days were not to come. The first transcontinental stagecoach reached San Francisco in a record-breaking run from St. Louis on 10 October, 1858 and changed the method of American transportation from East to West almost overnight.

The stagecoach and the possibility of overland travel hastened the demise of many remaining clippers. Some of them ended their days as coal hulks or cold-storage ships and were eventually broken up for scrap. Others did duty in the Civil War and were weighted and sunk for port barricades. Some were sold to British shipping lines and were used for a while on the Australian run. Still others caught fire and burned; or, waterlogged from so many voyages, sank or piled up on reefs. During its short life span, the American-built clipper ship was almost revered, not only by the greedy and often unscrupulous owners but by men everywhere who appreciated its beauty and seaworthiness. It was an inspiration for poets and artists wherever it was seen.

During the highly competitive days when there were too many fast ships and not enough cargo or passengers, shipping lines vied with one another to fill their vessels. Colorful cards were printed announcing the virtues of a particular ship and an impending departure. In those days a ship left port when its owners were satisfied that there was enough money involved to make a voyage worthwhile, and departure dates were never announced in advance. Other factors entering into the nebulous departure dates were the vicissitudes of weather and the increasing difficulty of finding a crew. In addition, it took time to purchase and stow a ship's stores and cargo.

A study of the sailing cards of the clipper ships reflects these variables. Clipper-ship cards were handed out to prospective passengers and cargo customers. They are perhaps the best record we have of the American extreme clipper and its owner's pride in announcing its many virtues. The cards were familiar advertisements in the 1860s and even later. Like most ephemeral paper items, few were kept, and those colorful cards that remain are highly prized by collectors of nautical items. However, any relics of clipper-ship days are eagerly sought and carefully preserved. They represent a highly romanticized and often infamous period of British and American maritime history.

The beauty of the clipper ships and the reverence in which they were held by their owners are evident in the names chosen for them. There seems to be no particular pattern in naming ships, and they were christened in a manner similar to that for racehorses. At least one ship, the *Dexter*, was called after a famous racehorse, and the sailing card advertising the *Dexter* has a copy of a popular Currier and Ives print of the well-known trotter. A name that connoted speed was appropriate to a clipper ship, and *Eagle Wing* was given to an extreme clipper built in Medford, Massachusetts. On a voyage from Boston to Bombay in 1865, the *Eagle Wing* disappeared and its fate has never been learned. Some clippers were named after famous persons in history or characters in literature. The *William Tell*, *Garibaldi*, *Don Quixote*, *Robin Hood*, *Hamlet* and *Ivanhoe* were all American clippers that brought treasure-seekers around the Horn in search of gold.

One clipper ship was named for the philanthropist and international banker George Peabody. He was born in Danvers, Massachusetts, and spent most of his adult life amassing a fortune, which he then gave away. He started life as an apprentice in the grocery business and rose to become so distinguished in London banking circles that when he died there was a public clamor in his adopted city for him to be buried in Westminster Abbey. He is mentioned here not only because of his clipper-ship namesake, but because some of his philanthropies have to do with the preservation of marine-related historical objects and records. He founded the Peabody Museum in Salem, Massachusetts, and the Peabody Institute in Baltimore, Maryland. He left money to Yale and Harvard universities for archeological and anthropological museums. He also provided housing for the poor in London that was known as "Peabody houses." The ship launched in Medford in 1854 carried the name of a highly respected man well known to the English-speaking world.

Many owners became somewhat poetic when it came to christening their ships. *Herald of the Morning, Nightingale, Romance of the Sea* and *Starlight* sailed along with more patriotically named ships such as the *Flying Eagle* or *Stars and Stripes.* The small cards that advertised the departure of one of these vessels with the poetic, patriotic or some other appealing name might not have been the decisive factor for a prospective passenger to· leave everything familiar behind him and take the expensive, uncomfortable and often hazardous journey 'round the Horn. But the clipper-ship cards that still exist give us some idea of the necessity for advertising and promoting the large number of sailing vessels which made these journeys.

8
CARVED
AND DECORATED
WHALEBONE OBJECTS

The story of the American whaling ships has been told in fiction, nonfiction, poetry and song for many years, but the most graphic record of the whaling days was left by the men who sailed the ships in search of the great whale. Small etchings on whales' teeth, scratched out with patience and care, represent an entire spectrum of the whaling man's interests, aspirations and activities. They also depict many of the popular illustrative subjects of the nineteenth century.

Although etching on whalebone is often thought of as an indigenous American folk art, there are some examples of similar work done by whaling men of other nations. Carving designs on tusks or bone is an ancient art that can be traced back as far as the eleventh century. That the practice became so widespread among American whalemen probably has to do with the fact that the American whaling fleet was so large and existed for such a long period. Also, it is probable that there was less literacy among the American whaling men, and they had fewer choices as to how to pass the many dreary hours aboard ship. There is little doubt that the art of scrimshaw became somewhat competitive and historical records attest to the fact that in at least one town, New Bedford, Massachusetts, prizes were given for the best examples of carved whalebone objects.

Whatever the reasons for the American whaling man's widespread pursuit of the art of scrimshaw, he seemed to develop his own subjects and style of carving and examples of his work are now highly prized by collectors of marine antiques everywhere. Although many forms of "busy work" have been found that can be attributed to talented sailors, the carved whalebone objects are high on the priority lists of nautical antique enthusiasts.

Scrimshaw, the term popularly used for carved whalebone art, is a word whose origins have been lost to us. However, it is useful as a verb describing the act of etching or engraving on whalebone and as a noun describing the work itself. There are references in whaling logs and journals to "skrimshander," "scrimshonter" and "scrimshorn," and a variety of spellings for these words can be found. The words originally referred to the ability to accomplish a small mechanical task neatly, and as nouns were used to describe scratched or carved work on any material. Today the derivative "scrimshaw" has only to do with the engraved art on whale's teeth or carved objects made of whalebone.

Scrimshaw, as a collectible object, has long been prized by those for whom the whaling industry holds a special meaning. In recent years, however, the demand for scrimshawed whale's teeth has in-

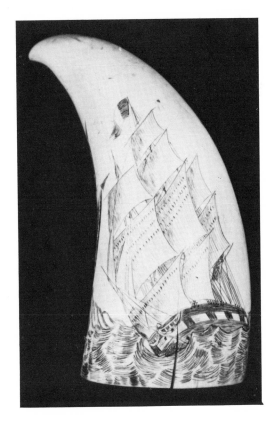

Whale's tooth engraved with a ship whose design fits the contour of the tooth amazingly well. SHELBURNE MUSEUM

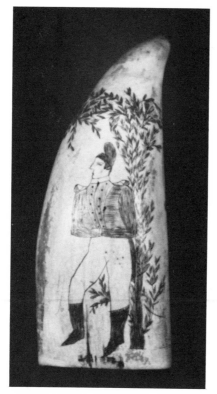

Carved whale's tooth with a soldier on one side and an American Indian on the other. SHELBURNE MUSEUM

creased to a point where prices are so high that genuinely old and good pieces are out of reach for all but the most affluent collectors. There are several reasons that scrimshaw has been "discovered" in recent years. Americans have begun to appreciate more and more the relatively few types of folk art that are indigenous to their country. The most highly prized scrimshaw examples are those with patriotic symbols and portraits of historical persons, or those that are engraved with whaling scenes.

It is probable that the art of scrimshaw would have become popular anyway among collectors of Americana by this time, but the art was given a great deal of attention during the administration of President John F. Kennedy. President Kennedy's love for the sea was well known, and he was given his first piece of scrimshaw by his wife while he was still in the United States Senate. This first acquisition led to the quiet collecting of more pieces of scrimshaw, which had as subjects ships, whaling scenes, and portraits and figures connected with American history. As knowledge of President Kennedy's interest in whalebone carvings spread, collectors and dealers became aware of the rising value of scrimshaw and purchased all they could find.

It is surprising that it took so long for American collectors, who have long prized other sea-related objects, to realize that the etched whales' teeth were among the most fascinating available objects within their field of interest. The whaling industry was so important in building the American economy prior to the Civil War that it should have been obvious to more than just a select few whaling historians and museum officials that any early whaling relics were worth preserving. The eighteenth-century whaling men played an important part in the early history of the United States. Were it not for the charts they made as they went farther and farther afield in search of the lucrative whale, it is doubtful that the American Navy

Carved whale's tooth depicting George Washington on horseback on one side and the American eagle and other patriotic devices on the other. Whaling scene continues around the bottom of the tooth. SHELBURNE MUSEUM

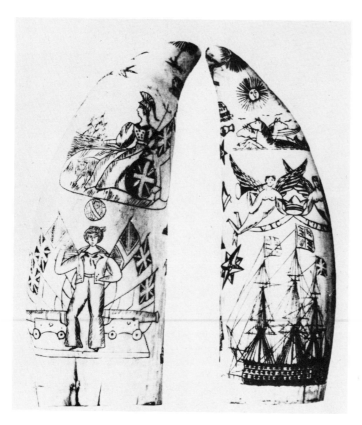

Whales' teeth deeply incised by a British sailor.
FLAYDERMAN COLLECTION

would have been so successful in the War of 1812. It is certainly no coincidence that so many early examples of etched whales' teeth have as subjects the heroes and ships of that war. Many of the craft that engaged in the sea battles were manned by the experienced sailors of the whaling vessels.

The teeth that were used for scrimshaw art came from the great sperm whales. These were hunted in the South Pacific by ships that traveled halfway around the world in pursuit of them. The voyages out of New Bedford, Nantucket, Sag Harbor and many other East Coast towns were long and tedious and often lasted as long as three years. The sailors had a lot of time on their hands. The careful filing, polishing and etching of a sperm whale's tooth helped to occupy those hours for New Englanders who had been brought up with the knowledge that idleness was a sin and that even leisure time had to be productive. Creating objects of beauty from whalebone seems to have been a major preoccupation for them, and the work they created gave them something to bring home after a long journey.

There was probably no shortage of material on which the whale-bone etcher could practice his art. Each sperm whale has about forty-two teeth. These were handed out to the members of a crew by the first mate and traded among them for other commodities that might be in short supply. Of course, the large, well-formed teeth were the most highly prized, and supply might have been a problem for the sailor who was especially prolific in the art of scrimshaw. In the history of American whaling it has been estimated that several million pieces of whalebone scrimshaw were decorated by American sailors. What is left today is obviously a small fraction of that amount.

In the *Golden Age of Whaling* Herman Melville tells us, "Throughout the Pacific, and also in Nantucket and New Bedford and Sag Harbor, you will come across lively sketches in whales and whaling scenes, graven by the fishermen themselves on Sperm whale-teeth, or ladies' busks wrought out of the Right whale-bone, and other skrimshander articles, as the whalemen call the numerous little ingenious contrivances they elaborately carve out of the rough material, in their hours of leisure. Some of them have dentistical-looking implements, especially intended for the skrimshandering business. But in general, they toil with their jack-knives alone; and with that omnipotent tool of the sailor, they will turn out anything you

Group of carved whalebone picks, three inches in length and made in a variety of shapes. SHELBURNE MUSEUM

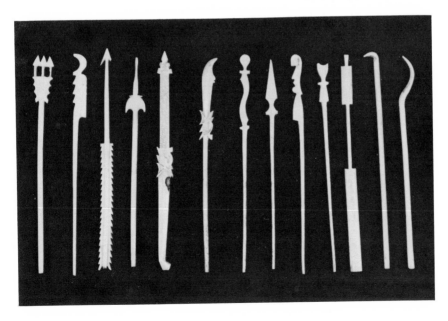

please in the way of a mariner's fancy."

The knife was indeed "omnipotent" for the whaling man. However, before the whale's tooth could be carved, pricked, or etched, the rough surface of the tooth had to be laboriously filed down and polished. The ridged tooth was first soaked in brine to soften it for filing. Shark's skin was often used for filing, as was sandpaper when available. All whaling ships had woodworking shops for ship repairs and for making containers in which to store whale oil, so that more elaborate tools than the sailor's jacknife were available to him if he needed them. There are many whalebone objects other than the decorated teeth that show obvious use of more sophisticated tools than the knife or needle. However, the decorated teeth were "pick-up" or "busywork," and the decorating was done by hand. The more time it took, the better.

Whale's teeth harden with age, but fresh ones are soft and more easily worked. The whaleman-artist usually penciled in a suitable design before he began etching a desired pattern. The designs varied enormously, but were not often original with the engraver. Those that are original are the most highly prized scrimshaw examples.

The designs were mostly derived from contemporary prints in magazines and books on board the ship and a popular source for female figures was *Godey's Ladies Book*, from which sailors copied fashion prints. The more talented whalemen drew their own pictures and these were usually scenes that were most familiar to them, such as their own ship and the small whaleboats in pursuit of the great whale. Spouting whales, churning water and the whaleman at work were popular subjects.

Patriotic motifs were also derived from existing prints. Portraits of American patriots were attempted with varying degrees of success by some scrimshaw artists. Subjects of a romantic nature were obvious choices of design for sailors for whom long absences away from home made the heart grow fond. Copies of portraits of loved ones at home were made from the daguerreotype pictures that were usually tucked into a sailor's sea chest after the middle of the nineteenth century. Other popular motifs were derived from a ship's sternboard carvings or figurehead. Rope designs, diamond or star or heart shapes, anchors, ships' wheels and the compass rose were also used.

Once the penciled design was etched on the surface of the tooth, the lines and pricks made by knife point or other pointed tools were brought out by rubbing in any coloring agent available on shipboard. Everything from tobacco juice to ink or soot was used for this purpose. Paint and dye were also used when a more varied palette was desired. The tooth was then subjected to many more hours of vigorous rubbing and polishing.

While the American whaleman spent longer periods at sea as the sperm whale became more and more elusive, the voyages of their British counterparts were of somewhat shorter duration, and discipline on British ships was probably more regimented. Less time was spent at scrimshaw, and examples of British carved whale's teeth are quite scarce today. The British whaling fleet was much smaller than that of America, and the art was not as popular among English whalers. Therefore, carved whales' teeth with obvious British provenance are in high demand by collectors of marine antiques. Extant British scrimshaw examples are of high quality, and it is probable that only whalemen with some artistic leanings bothered to pursue the hobby. Many whale's teeth were brought home undecorated by British whaling men and sent to silversmiths to be made into silver- or gold-mounted snuffboxes and other small objects.

It should be noted that not all existing decorated whale's teeth were made on board ship. Early in the eighteenth century, landbound craftsmen in American seaport towns purchased whatever ivory was available to use for carving decorative or useful objects that they could sell. Certainly, a great many retired whaling men continued their art on land. However, it is generally felt that most old whalebone carvings made with nautical motifs were the work of sailors on board ship.

While there was undoubtedly an ample supply of whales' teeth for the sailor to engrave, supplies were traded with the Eskimos for walrus tusks, which were engraved in a similar manner. The long spiral tusks of the narwhal whale was considered a price piece of ivory, and canes and other objects were fashioned from them.

Although the decorated teeth of the whale have now become highly desirable objects for the collector, there are, of course, many other objects made from whalebone that are also eagerly sought. Most of these whalebone novelties and useful objects were fashioned by the same whalemen, and many show an ingenuity in carving and fashioning useful and decorative pieces that represent an obvious investment in time, talent and patience.

The list of carved whalebone objects is long and the variety of shapes and adaptations to be found in a single category is enormous.

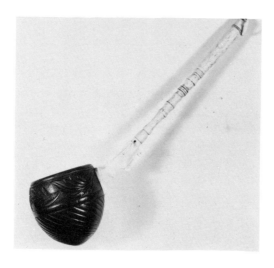

Dipper made on board a whaler from carved coconut shell and whalebone. SHELBURNE MUSEUM

For instance, pie-crimping wheels, or jagging wheels, used for cutting and decorating piecrust, can be found in limitless shapes and sizes. The small carved wheels with movable parts were made in such variety as to indicate that the whalemen who made them were skilled at their art and were bound by no rules in pursuing it.

Pie crimpers seem to be the most abundant single object carved in whalebone. Many of the crimpers were made to serve more than one purpose in pastry preparation. A two-pronged fork for piercing crust was often attached to the crimper. Another appendage might be a stamp with reverse lettering for outlining a message on cookie or pie dough.

Motifs used for the pierced or etched designs on the handles of the crimpers also show a great deal of ingenuity and imagination. In some crimpers the wheel is an integral part of the design. One example illustrates a figure riding a unicycle with the crimping wheel serving as the cycle. Handles were also carved in the shape of a human arm with the fist holding the piercing fork. Seahorses, seagulls, fish and whales are other carved three-dimensional shapes for crimper handles.

All motifs that figured in American folk art of the late eighteenth and nineteenth centuries can be found in the designs of the pie crimpers. The heart, diamond, star, cross, flower and leaf shapes are all evident in whalebone-carved pie crimpers. Some crimper handles were decorated with horn or shells, and others have baleen decora-

78

tion. Crimpers have been found with up to seven different-size wheels attached.

One can only surmise today why there seems to be such an abundance of whalebone pie crimpers. Obviously, whalebone carvers were competitive in attempting to make artistic and imaginative objects. It is also probable that whalemen on ship's rations looked forward with great anticipation to the homemade pies they would have when their long journey was over. The crimpers were obviously welcome gifts for wives, mothers and sweethearts, and in the New England folk art tradition the utensil was useful as well as decorative.

A great many other functional and decorative objects for household use were made of whalebone. The list is almost endless and shows the desire of the sailor to bring home practical gifts. Clothespins, rolling pins, cookie presses, mortars and pestles, forks, knives, napkin rings, candlesticks, brush handles, doorknobs, picture frames and many other objects were fashioned for household use.

Evidence that the women left alone in home port were frequently on the minds of the whalers can be found in the abundance of needleworking tools that were made from whalebone. While the sailors used their busywork to allay boredom on the ship, their wives' lonesome evenings were occupied by the various forms of needlework that kept their hands and minds occupied in a constructive manner. Husbands, lovers, sons and brothers supplied many of the tools the seaport women needed for sewing, knitting, hooking, crocheting and darning.

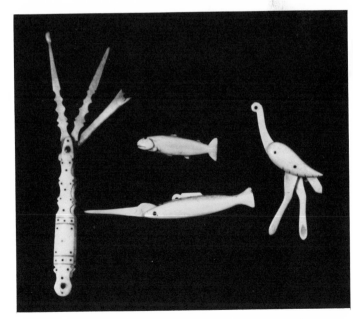

The pocket piece on the left has toothpick, ear cleaner and toothbrush. The long-beaked bird on the right is for cleaning teeth or nails, while bird's feet are ear cleaners. SHELBURNE MUSEUM

Baleen ditty box with an American ship engraved on the lid. FLAYDERMAN COLLECTION

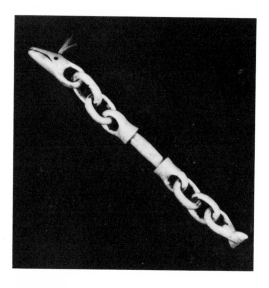

This clever chain, in the shape of a whale, is carved from one solid piece of whalebone. The "spout" is made of bristles. SHELBURNE MUSEUM

Tableswift in closed position, on whalebone and wood stand. SHELBURNE MUSEUM

The most complicated and painstaking object made of whalebone in the category of needlecraft aids is the tableswift, used for holding hanks of yarn being wound into a ball. The swift was a particularly useful tool for the wife whose husband was seldom around to provide two willing hands for this task. The swifts were comprised of many flat stick-shaped ribs tied together with string or fastened with wire at the joints and folded up when not in use. Many of the swifts were made with clamps that fastened them to the table edge. Others had more elaborate bases with drawers to hold sewing implements and spokes for spools of thread.

Elaborate sewing boxes, many of them oval in shape and joined with lappers that make them reminiscent of the Shaker boxes of the nineteenth century, were also formed of whalebone. Some of these were delicately etched with whaling scenes and other designs. Thimbles, sewing birds, crochet hooks, knitting needles, darning eggs, measuring sticks, button hooks, buttons, needle holders and pincushion holders were other sewing implements designed by the whaling men as gifts to take home. Some of the larger items were made in a combination of materials. There was no shortage of seashell for inlay in the South Pacific, and tropical wood was also combined with whale ivory for many of these objects.

The most personal of all gifts brought by the whaling man to his wife or sweetheart is the decorated busk used as a stay in the front center of corsets in the nineteenth century. The busks were made of

Three incised and brightly colored whalebone busks for use in front center of corsets. SHELBURNE MUSEUM

tropical wood, the panbone of the sperm whale or a piece of baleen. They were usually heavily decorated with etched and colorful designs. It is interesting that one of the major products of the whale that brought great profits to the shipowners was whalebone sold to commercial corsetmakers. However, the whaling man's wife or sweet-

Baleen corset busk engraved with designs of churches, hearts, trees and the American flag. SHELBURNE MUSEUM

heart owned a handmade, hand-decorated whalebone busk that undoubtedly reminded her all day of her loved one.

Motifs for the hand-crafted corset busks were enormously varied and often contained pictures or messages of a more personal nature than other scrimshawed objects. Hearts and flowers were always prevalent, and the top of the busk was frequently cut in a heart shape. The whaling men were not averse to using less suitable designs if they thought it might remind their loved ones of them when they were on the high seas. They often etched their own portraits on the surfaces of the busks; pictures of whales and ships and sometimes even patriotic motifs. The verse "When this you see, Remember me" was carved into many busks along with symbols of nature that reminded the sailor of home. Flowers, fruit, trees, butterflies and birds were also motifs for busk decoration and, oddly enough, the funereal symbols typical of the nineteenth century have also been found. With one of these handsome, but stiff and obviously uncomfortable, strips of whalebone poking into her diaphragm each day, it is unlikely that the beloved of any whaling man would be apt to forget him.

On every whaling ship there were many men who had no one waiting at home, since it was common for the nineteenth-century sailor to have as few ties to land as possible. These men, and perhaps many who did have families, occupied their time and talents making objects for use on the ships. It is probable that the ships' carpenters also fashioned some of the whalebone embellishments for their vessels. Some whaling ships were profusely equipped with a variety of carved whalebone objects. Fids for ropework were made and sometimes decorated with the owner's name or initials. A variety of tools for the sailmaker was made, and handles for other ships' tools were carved from whalebone. Lures, mallets, measuring sticks, seam rubbers and the aforementioned whale stamps for keeping the logbooks are only a few of the useful objects the sailors made for their own use.

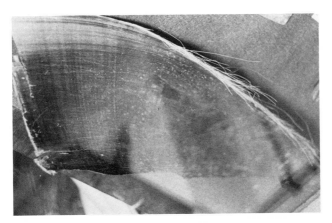

Left: Piece of baleen, the tough, fibrous plates that serve as strainers for food in mouths of right whales and some other types of whale. Sailors used this material in their craft. SUFFOLK COUNTY WHALING MUSEUM *Right: Baleen ditty box, three inches in diameter, made of strip of baleen riveted at the seam. Top and base are of wood. Baleen circle inlaid in lid.* SHELBURNE MUSEUM

Ditty box made of wood and baleen, inlaid with shell and whalebone. FLAYDERMAN COLLECTION

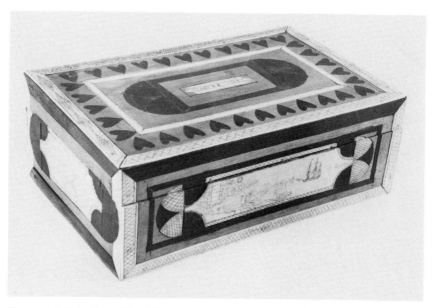

*Box made for Lucy Francis out of a variety of exotic wood
and inlaid with engraved whalebone.* FLAYDERMAN COLLEC-
TION

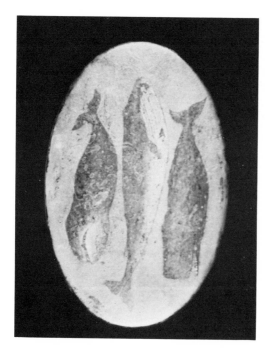

*Whaleman's ditty box of
painted iron with etched
whales on the lid.* SHEL-
BURNE MUSEUM

At least one sailor carved and etched the keys, bridge and tailpiece for his violin. Canes, knife handles, needle cases and vises were also made, and the truly ambitious model ship builder used whale ivory in place of wood to fashion parts of his ships.

Ditty boxes of whalebone or baleen, often in combination with wood, were made for the sailors' own use, and other boxes in this combination of materials were made as homecoming gifts. Cane heads were frequently carved from whalebone, and the shapes are as unlimited as the whaling man's imagination. Ladies' legs, bent at the knee, the clenched fist seen also in pie crimpers and other carved objects, animal or bird heads or complete bodies, rope knot shapes familiar to the sailor and many other delicately carved cane knobs were made. These were frequently applied to polished wood canes made from the exotic trees of the South Pacific islands.

Watch holders were made of wood in the shape of elaborate churches or in replica of a town hall or other municipal building entrenched in the memory of the carver. These wooden structures

Group of cane heads, many of which are of carved whalebone. Note lady's leg and animal heads. SUFFOLK COUNTY WHALING MUSEUM

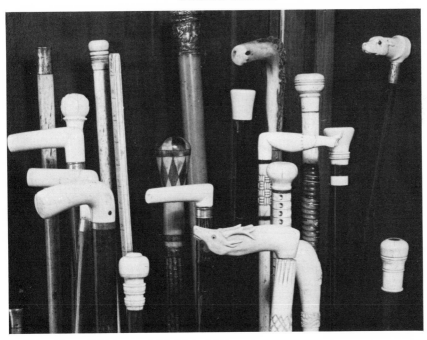

Left: Watch holder, 14½ inches high, made of wood and whalebone around 1850. Right: Domino set in carved and incised box with sliding top, together with two brightly colored snuffboxes.
BOTH PHOTOS: SHELBURNE MUSEUM

were then embellished with whalebone decoration. There are some rare examples of elaborate watch holders made entirely of panbone of the whale.

Lest it be thought that only practical objects were carved, it should be noted that games of dominoes, cribbage boards, game counters and dice were also made. A few full-dimensional figure groups have been found, and miniature whales were also made. Toys and dolls were carved, and some of the dollhouse miniatures have remarkable detail and proportions. Doll furniture and children's games and learning devices are also examples of scrimshaw made for missed offspring and favorite nieces and nephews. These gifts were one way of keeping the memory of an absent father or uncle alive during his several years' voyage.

While the art of decorating whalebone was not indigenous to

American whaling men, it was certainly widely practiced among the crewmen and officers of the whaling fleets of America. Scrimshaw rescued the seamen from the desperate hours when, without his piece of bone and his knife, he would have had nothing to do.

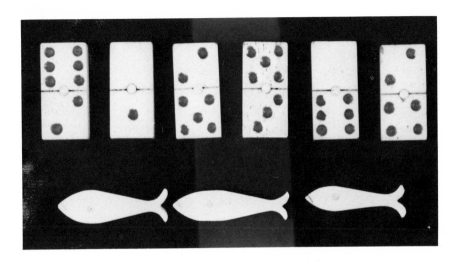

Whalebone dominoes and fish-shaped game counters. SHELBURNE MUSEUM *Below: This whaleman's fiddle has had its neckpiece and pegs replaced with scrimshawed whalebone—one of the rarest uses of American scrimshaw that has yet been found.* FLAYDERMAN COLLECTION

9
SHIP MODELS

The lover of the sea collects his ships in the only practical form available, and there is no collector of marine antiques who does not own or search for at least one model of a sailing ship. The designers and builders of ships as well as their crews have always made them, and the entire history of the architecture of shipbuilding can be found in these miniature vessels.

While many of the builders' models of famous sailing ships are in the possession of the governments that ordered the full-size ships constructed, many others are in private hands. In recent years a few important models of great historical significance have come on the market to be purchased at increasingly high prices by collectors.

Models of Egyptian boats built as early as 2500 B.C. have been found in tombs. They were included among other riches to ensure a fast journey to the Beyond for the soul of the departed. Votive models that represent the early Mediterranean trade ships have also been found in churches. The tradition of making models to serve as votive instruments has continued through many centuries in ports where the survival of a village depends upon the safe return of its ships and men.

The models that are most avidly sought by today's collectors are those that represent the great days of the sailing ships. The brigs, frigates and barks of the early days are sought by collectors all over the world, little thought being given to the nationality of the ships. Spanish galleons; French, English and American men-of-war; early Dutch trading ships; the packet boats of the nineteenth century; and the magnificent clipper ships have all been reproduced. Collectors

Bone model of a Baltimore schooner made by an American incarcerated in Dartmoor Prison, England, during the War of 1812. Resting on superbly made straw-work and bone base, this is a rare example of a documented American-made model of this type. FLAYDERMAN COLLECTION

Votive model of Spanish galleon of the early sixteenth century, measuring fifty-four inches in length. Found in an ancient chapel near Burgos, Spain.

are well aware that each sailing ship had its own individual shape, rigging and personality, and that the models that outlasted the ships they represent are all important documentation of world shipping history. In many cases the existing models are the only record we have that certain ships ever existed. Builders' models of ships were made for many ships that were never ordered.

The building of an accurate ship model has always been a painstaking task, one that requires infinite patience and complete knowledge of how ships are constructed and how they work. All carving, sailmaking and rigging—before the day of the convenient do-it-yourself kit—had to be done by hand. This required the use of ingenuity in making the variety of ship's hardware and fittings in miniature. By the beginning of this century, model-making had become a popular hobby, and books and articles were published giving the modelmaker some direction as to how to adapt materials at hand to his purposes. Previous to this, sailors learned model-making from one another and used materials easily available to them in carpenter's shops aboard ship or in port in order to fashion models that had some degree of authenticity.

Whalemen could while away the hours aboard ship carving the whalebone that was available to them. Sailors and officers aboard

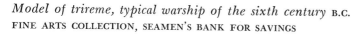

Model of trireme, typical warship of the sixth century B.C.
FINE ARTS COLLECTION, SEAMEN'S BANK FOR SAVINGS

Above: Model of American frigate, U.S.S. Essex. FINE ARTS COLLECTION, SEAMEN'S BANK FOR SAVINGS

Right: Model of HMS Siren, *64 guns, circa 1750. The ornate bow is heavily carved, and the figurehead a gilt carving of Mars.*

naval and merchant vessels seemed to use some of the small amount of leisure time available to them carving hulls, sewing sails and arranging authentic rigging of replicas of the ships they sailed. Hundreds of hours might easily have been taken up with the building of a model. And often, in these sailor-made models, every effort was

Half model of a British warship of the latter half of the seventeenth century, showing timber arrangement under skin. NEW YORK YACHT CLUB

made to reproduce the authentic structure of a ship.

The truly authentic ship models that exist today were made by the architects and builders of ships and were meant to be more than attractive ornaments for a library. While many of these builders' models are now in museums, one spectacular example is owned by the New York Yacht Club and has a particularly interesting history. It was found for sale in Europe by the architect Stanford White, who collected ship models. He sold it to J. Pierpont Morgan, who presented it to the Yacht Club at the beginning of this century. When the Yacht Club attempted to identify the model, it became evident that it was "one which escaped retention in England at the time when, by order of His Majesty William IV, the models at Kensington Palace were transferred in 1830 to the Naval College at Greenwich."

As with some other British shipbuilders' models, the one owned by the New York Yacht Club is left skinless on one side to exhibit the method of timber construction. It is a model of a British warship of the latter half of the seventeenth century, and the stem and stern-post construction can be easily studied.

An important collection of British ship models can be seen in the National Maritime Museum in Greenwich, England, and in the United States there is another outstanding collection on view at the Naval Academy in Annapolis, Maryland.

All ships of historical importance were copied as models many times, and the demise of a ship that had long outlived its seaworthiness was no reason for model-makers to stop reproducing her in miniature. Documented models made by the captain or a crew member who revered his own ship enough to copy her in miniature are, of course, desirable items for any model collector. Any old, well-made model of a ship, even though its maker is not recorded, is also highly thought of. Authenticity of line and detail are the important factors in determining the value of an old ship model. In some cases the model builders went to the trouble of consulting original plans and

Model of American privateer, Rattlesnake. FINE ARTS COL-LECTION, SEAMEN'S BANK FOR SAVINGS

Above: Model of an eighteenth-century Spanish frigate with carved and gilded quarter and stern galleries, figurehead and gunports. All sails are set and she mounts 24 guns.

drawings in order to make their work as accurate as possible.

A well-made, detailed ship model is to the collector what a carefully outfitted scale model dollhouse is to a child. It is a starting place for fantasies of a bygone era where the beauty of billowing sails, the danger of hurricanes and pirates, the anticipation of sea battles and the lure of far-off lands can place one temporarily in another world. A British man-of-war complete with retractable guns and decorated with a carved, latticed and balustered high stern and carrying carvings of the British coat of arms and carved sea nymphs is more than just a remarkable thirty-inch example of handwork and detail. To own it is to have the ability to fantasize one's self back to the middle of the eighteenth century, to imagine climbing the masts, repairing the rigging and manning the cannons. The glory and strength of the British navy in the eighteenth century can be better understood by

Left: Boxwood scale model of HMS Majestic *with 102 guns, circa 1785. Lower hull covered with copper sheets and trimmed with baleen. Carved with warriors, sea nymphs and British coat of arms. Ivory figurehead of full-standing figure of Roman warrior.*

Right: Model of American bark, Great Republic. FINE ARTS COLLECTION, SEAMEN'S BANK FOR SAVINGS

studying the complexities of its ships than by reading the dry pages of its history.

Ship models exist today that were made during the War of 1812 to represent the famous craft of that era. The vessels of the Napoleonic Wars can still be found in model size. A reproduction of the U.S. brig *Hornet*, for instance, recalls many important battles, such as its encounter with the *Penguin* when Captain Biddle was wounded.

Model of Frigate, U.S.S. *Hartford.* FINE ARTS COLLECTION, SEAMEN'S BANK FOR SAVINGS

Model of HM *Brig* Nereus, *circa 1820, admiralty boxwood construction.*

The *Hornet's* escape in April 1815 from a British seventy-four-gun vessel in San Salvador, recalls a fascinating episode of American and British naval history. It was upon arriving at San Salvador that Captain Biddle learned that peace had been declared between the United States and Great Britain. If contemporary marine paintings and prints tell us more clearly what a particular sea battle looked like, it is through a study of the models of the actual ships that took part in the battles that our imaginations are further fired.

Every type of boat or ship that was ever made can be found in ship model collections. We can study the similarities and differences in national styles and methods of shipbuilding used by all the civilizations of the world. Eskimo kayaks and Chinese junks have been reproduced in miniature. Few yachtsmen of the nineteenth or twentieth century have not owned scale models of the expensive craft in which they sailed.

From early times models of ships have been made by the shipbuilders in order to entice an order from a government or private shipping interest. When naval architecture became a science in the seventeenth century, it was common practice for a model to be made in advance of the construction of a ship. As a result, there are many existing models of ships that were never built or were so modified in their construction as to differ in many details from these original models.

Models of all historic ships have been made in the past and will probably always be made as long as there are craftsmen with the infinite patience necessary to make them. Most certainly, the ships that changed the course of history of many seafaring nations deserve to be reproduced in miniature. The longships of the Vikings, the ships of the Barbary pirates, those of the Portuguese explorers and the merchant vessels of the Venetians have all been made into scale models since they first sailed the seas. Antonio's fleet of Argosies in Shakespeare's *The Merchant of Venice* was not a figment of the bard's imagination, and these great ships were once responsible for making the city of Venice the wonder of the world. Magnificently ornamented, they were referred to as "the pageants of the sea" by Salarino. Model-makers once reproduced this grandeur in miniature to embellish the furnishings of palaces.

If the caravels of Christopher Columbus of Genoa changed the course of history and geography, his three famous ships have appealed to model-makers' imaginations for centuries. The three bluff-

Bone model of the Charles W. Morgan, *last surviving ship of American whaling fleet.* FINE ARTS COLLECTION, SEAMEN'S BANK FOR SAVINGS

bowed vessels with a double castle in the stern and a single castle at the bow were ships that were little improved over those of the early Christian era. The *Santa María,* the largest of the three, has frequently been fashioned in miniature by model-makers. She was about one hundred tons and measured only ninety feet from bow to stern. With three masts and a bowsprit, she carried square sails on the fore and main masts and a lateen sail on the mizzenmast. The deck amidships was low, and about one fourth the distance aft it dropped down abruptly. Near the stern another deck arose to about the height of the forward deck, and behind this was reared a high sterncastle. Since there are no precise records of these ships, all models are part fantasy.

Any American schoolchild can identify Columbus's ships from the most amateur of models. The other two ships, the *Pinta* and the *Niña,* were considerably smaller, the former being fifty tons and the latter only forty. The exploits of these three small ships are well known and have been romanticized throughout the history of America to the point that fact can hardly be strained from fiction. It is fact, however, that the *Santa María* was run upon a sandbar through the inexperience and carelessness of a teen-aged helmsman, and that she sank off the coast of Haiti. Current efforts to retrieve what is left of the *Santa María* might give future model-makers more information as to what the ship really looked like.

The English, Dutch and French merchant ships of the fifteenth, sixteenth and seventeenth centuries that have been noted for the exploits of their captains and crews have all been reproduced over and over by expert and amateur model builders. John Cabot's *Matthew*—which reached the shore of what was thought to be the coast of China in 1498, but which was, in reality, the coast of North America —has been built in model size many times. The *Half Moon* (*Halve Moen*) of Henry Hudson—a three-masted ship with a sharp, sheer fore and aft, a narrow high stern, a short and rather high forecastle and a main deck that was as wide as it was long—found its way, after many trials, to the river now named for him in the State of New York. Many models of this famous ship were built in celebration of the three hundredth anniversary in 1909 of Hudson's exploits in the *Half Moon.*

Less attention has been given to Hudson's other ship, *Discovery,* on which he set out to search further for a northwest passage. This voyage turned out to be a tragic and futile journey. The mutinous

Model of Henry Hudson's ship, the Half Moon, *constructed by the builders of a replica of the ship which was a feature of the Hudson-Fulton celebration in New York in 1909.* NEW YORK YACHT CLUB

crew that had been quartered in the Arctic with insufficient supplies set Hudson, his son, the ship's carpenter and seven crew members adrift in a small boat. Hudson's Bay became the explorer's tomb.

Official models of ships were made in England from 1649, when the Admiralty Committee issued an order asking builders to "present models of the frigotts they severally undertake." The scale models, complete with figureheads and carvings, were collected as ornaments as soon as they became available. It should be noted by today's collector that the builders' models are by far the most desirable of all ship models. Although there are many models built by seamen who loved their ships, there were few occasions when a ship was seen out of water by these men, and their understanding of the shape and design of the hull often lacked the correct proportions. The sails and rigging are usually accurate, however, for the details of these would be familiar to every seaman.

The Elizabethan ships of the famous "sailors of Devon" have historic and romantic connotations and have been reproduced by modelmakers for centuries. The Queen's ships, rich from their voyages to the New World and having laid claim to vast new territories, defied the might of Spain. The *Minion* and *Jesus* of Sir John Hawkins and Sir Francis Drake's *Judith, Pascha* and *Swan*—and especially the

101

Model of American clipper ship Sovereign of the Seas. FINE
ARTS COLLECTION, SEAMEN'S BANK FOR SAVINGS

Model of American clipper ship Flying Cloud. FINE ARTS
COLLECTION, SEAMEN'S BANK FOR SAVINGS

Golden Hind in which Drake circled the globe—are all ships that recall a prosperous era in England's sea history.

The ships that founded the territory in the New World that was called "Virginia" were sent by another Devonian, Sir Walter Raleigh. Although he did not sail in them, he was responsible for dispatching a company of settlers on the *Revenge* under the command of Sir Richard Grenville, another son of Devon, and a colony was founded on Roanoke Island. The homesick colonists soon returned to England. The *Revenge* is also well known for its great battle with the Spanish fleet. The sea adventurers of Devon will always be remembered, and the ships sailed by these men will be reproduced in miniature as long as there are model-makers and collectors.

By comparing the existing models of early ships we can see the advances made in ship design over the centuries. From the rather clumsy proportions of the early brigs and frigates to the sleek lines of the American extreme clippers, it is possible to see the sailing ship being adapted from convertible warships to vessels built only for speed and passenger and trade service.

Models of fishing craft from all parts of the world have also been

Model of the whaling ship Jefferson. SUFFOLK COUNTY WHALING MUSEUM

made, and many of these are completely accurate in detail and proportions. Whaling ships, of such importance to the economy of New England, have been reproduced in miniature, as have the whaleboats they carried. Most of the whaling ship models were made by the men who sailed on them, and frequently models can be found that are at least part whalebone.

Bone ships of another sort have come down to us from the Napoleonic Wars. These were made by French prisoners of war in England to relieve their boredom and, by selling them to their captors in the crowded English prisons, to earn some money to supplement their rations. Some of these ships, made of animal bone, are miniatures of French naval vessels, but adorned with British flags and given the names of well-known British ships.

Within the category of model collecting there are many specializations. Ships of national historical interest are collected in every seafaring country. Ships with local associations, bone ships made by prisoners of war, naval vessels, and even the later steamships and ferryboats are sought. Ships carved and rigged by known model-

Detail of model of American whaling ship illustrates great
fidelity to scale in rigging and miniature replicas of parts.
FINE ARTS COLLECTION, SEAMEN'S BANK FOR SAVINGS

Balancing ships-in-bottles. FINE ARTS COLLECTION, SEAMEN'S
BANK FOR SAVINGS

makers are all prize collectors' items today. Many collectors search only for models made contemporaneously with the ships they represent, while others are content to purchase later reproductions. Half-hull ship models as well as fully rigged ship models are currently in high demand. Although sailor-made models are less realistic, they have a charm of their own. Those with panoramic backgrounds and blue putty waves are colorful and charming decorative objects that remind us of the sailor's love for his ship.

There seems to have been no shortage of glass bottles aboard most ships. Along with provisions brought on a journey for nightly rations of rum or whiskey for the crew, more than one seabag or sailor's chest was carried aboard with a private stock for emergencies, or simply to help a sailor through the lonely hours. Sailors were not known for their sobriety, and by the nineteenth century men on shore were often plied with liquor in order to get them on board without resistance.

Encouraging sailors to imbibe on shore with the goal of collecting a crew was common practice in America at the start of the nineteenth century. Many American privateers were furnished at least in part with crews who had been enticed by the "rendezvous," or party, at the local waterfront tavern. The tab for the rendezvous was picked up by the shipowner and was usually not inconsiderable. Existing invoices of the tavernkeepers for expenses incurred in these recruiting parties attest to the fact that the American sailor's thirst for glory and adventure did not outweigh his thirst for punch, grog and toddy.

Ship built into pocket flask is anchored in putty sea and has background panorama of lighthouse and rocks. FINE ARTS COLLECTION, SEAMEN'S BANK FOR SAVINGS

Drinking aboard ship in the eighteenth and nineteenth centuries seems to have been regarded with varying degrees of tolerance. Sometimes drinking was controlled to some extent by doling out a ration of rum at mealtime. At other times it appears that a need for alcohol could lead to disastrous results. The log of Francis Boardman, captain of the sloop *Adventure*, has this revealing final entry for a return voyage from the West Indies to Salem in 1774:

> The end of this Voyage for wich I am very Thankfull on Acct. of a Grate Deal of Truble by a bad mate. his name is William Robson of Salem, he was Drunk most Part of the Voyage.

Since this was Captain Boardman's first voyage as master of a ship, it is possible that he learned from this experience to choose his first mates more carefully on ensuing voyages.

An especially appealing collector's item in the category of marine antiques is the sailor-made ship-in-a-bottle. If written directions for this fascinating folk art were available in the nineteenth century, they would probably begin "Step one: Empty one large glass bottle."

The blown glass bottles that have been found by marine archeologists in many early shipwrecks are collectors' items in themselves. Too few of these square case gin bottles or round mold-turned bottles have survived to satisfy the collectors of early blown glass. However, for the collector of marine antiques, a bottle with a small model of a sailing ship or panorama of a seaport village inside it is of greater interest. This method of keeping occupied at sea by using available materials to make a decorative product required great patience and skill.

The ships and other subjects built into old bottles by sailors and waterfront hobbyists are in great demand today. Many seem to have been the work of mid-nineteenth-century sailors. As with most folk

Elaborate wood, bone and string puzzles-in-bottles, made by American sailors in the eighteenth century.
,THE PEABODY MUSEUM

art of the seaman, there seem to be few records of the makers of these models, but it is probable that they were mainly British and American sailors. Many of the ship models of this type are crude, for the method of building a ship that would fit through the mouth of a bottle precluded technical perfection.

The procedure for inserting a ship into a bottle was to build a tiny model, frequently of a clipper ship, cutting off the hull a little below the waterline. It was necessary to make the hull slender enough to pass through the mouth of the bottle. The hull could not be larger than half the space allotted at the bottle mouth. The hull was then painted and varnished and hollowed out from the bottom. The realism of the hull depended upon the skill and patience of the model-maker, and frequently deckhouses, lifeboats and steering gear were included. The masts were then added, folded down against the hull and rigged with thread with ends long enough to extend through the bottle's mouth after the ship had been inserted to pull the mast upright.

Ship-in-bottle has elaborate rigging attached to nails on stand. Sails can be manipulated from outside of bottle. Stand is combination of ship's wheel and anchor motifs.
FINE ARTS COLLECTION, SEAMEN'S BANK FOR SAVINGS

Once the tiny ship had been built and rigged, blue or green putty was placed in the side of the bottle and the ship was pushed through the neck of the bottle and embedded into the putty. The sailor made his own tools for this work, and usually a long hooked wire was the main instrument. The wire was used to push the masts into an upright position. The thread ends were held outside the bottle's mouth, wound around the neck of the bottle and glued into place. If paper sails were to be added, these were fitted and glued to the yards before the ship was inserted into the bottle. The paper sails were then rolled up for insertion. After the ship had been placed and the putty hardened, the sails were hasped by heating the metal wire in boiling water and pushing the centers of the paper sails to give them shape and a realistic windblown appearance.

Although the sailor who undertook this complicated form of busywork needed a great deal of patience to achieve a satisfactory finished product, there are even more complicated forms of this peculiar folk art. Within some nineteenth-century bottles there are entire seaport towns reproduced in miniature with the use of putty, paint and wooden sticks. Lighthouses, trees, rocks, houses and one or more ships form tiny waterfront scenes. Scenes of the Crucifixion have been found, as well as strange and complicated forms of "puzzle work." The latter seems to be an early form of the art, and a group of these bottles with strange interior sculptures of bone, wood and string can be seen in the Peabody Museum in Salem, Massachusetts.

The many variations of bottle art made by seamen have now become quite scarce. The type most frequently found is the neatly made clipper ship, fitted horizontally into its green putty sea. Many of these horizontal bottles rest in handmade wooden cradles. The collector should be warned, however, that a great many ships-in-bottles were made well into this century, when "how-to" books and articles were published for land-bound hobbyists. There are some forms of this art being practiced today and to avoid purchasing a late example, it is necessary to study the types of bottles made and used before the end of the nineteenth century, when machine-made bottles came into use. The age of a bottle is not always a clue to the age of the model built in it, but at least it helps to know if the bottle itself is old.

Ships and other subjects built into bottles by nineteenth-century sailors are among the most colorful of all hand-made sailors' art and well documented examples should be carefully preserved.

10
SHIP COMMEMORATIVES, NAUTICAL AWARDS AND PRESENTATIONS

It is an expensive endeavor to preserve an entire ship, and very few vessels of important historical associations have been allowed to remain intact. A few ships of the sailing era have been restored as national historical monuments or museum attractions, but the initial efforts that were required to keep the sailing craft from oblivion have often been made by individuals rather than governments. One would have to travel a distance to visit more than a couple of these historical relics that survived dismantling.

In cases where a ship of great historical importance has been saved, it has been customary to raise money to pay for the restoration by selling relics as souvenirs. These are all collectors' items today and can be found in a variety of forms.

Perhaps the most notable of all warship commemoratives are those made from parts of the *Victory*, the flagship of Admiral Lord Nelson. Nelson's famous battle at Trafalgar was fought on 21 October, 1805. The Spanish and French combined fleets of thirty-three sails of the line and seven frigates outnumbered the British fleet of twenty-seven sails of the line and four frigates. From the *Victory*, Nelson commanded the attack in two lines at right angles to the enemy, and completely defeated them. Nelson was mortally wounded at the moment of victory, but his decisiveness and bravery put an end

An oak box with gold mounts presented by the City of Bath to Cdr. William E. Parry, Royal Navy, for his discoveries in Polar regions. The box, made of oak from Parry's ship Hecla, *was presented in 1821.* FLAYDERMAN COLLECTION

Nelson commemorative box made from quarterdeck plank of Victory, *with engraved silver medallion on lid.* FLAYDER-MAN COLLECTION

Desk ornament made of wood from Nelson's flagship, the Victory. FLAYDERMAN COLLECTION

Piece of wood from the Victory *presented to Burnham Thorpe, Admiral Lord Nelson's birthplace.* FLAYDERMAN COLLECTION

to Napoleon's plans for invading England and established British supremacy of the seas for one hundred years following Trafalgar.

Nelson's ship, the *Victory*, has been preserved as a national monument at Portsmouth, England, but pieces of her are now to be found in many parts of the world. A great many tributes to Lord Nelson's accomplishments have been made from parts of his flagship removed during restoration. The amazing thing is that the ship exists at all after contributing to the many small boxes and other commemorative objects made from her hull!

112

Among the relics of the *Victory* illustrated here is a box made from the quarterdeck plank, a wooden anchor ornament and a piece of wood presented by the Lords of the Admiralty to Burnham Thorpe, where Horatio Nelson was born.

When the wreck of the H.M.S. *Royal George* was raised at Spithead after having rested in a watery grave since sinking in 1782, a great many commemorative souvenirs were made from its hull.

Box made from part of a beam from HMS *Royal George.*
FLAYDERMAN COLLECTION

Left: Box made of wood from HMS *Royal George. Right: Box commemorating* HMS *Victory.* FLAYDERMAN COLLECTION

Wood inkwell in shape of a capstan and a book-shaped box (standing) commemorating HMS *Royal George. The small book is covered with wood from the ship and tells the story of her loss.* FLAYDERMAN COLLECTION

Inkwells, miniature cannon and half-hull models were carved and identified with suitably engraved plaques that gave the tragic history of the ship. Miniature books with covers made from planks of the *Royal George* recounted the story of the sinking. They were entitled *A concis account of the Loss of the Royal George at Spithed—1782,* and the first edition was obviously so successful that its publisher, W. H. Charpentier, issued a second.

While the *Victory* is the one early warship that has been preserved in England, Americans have their historic naval preservation in the *Constitution,* the only American frigate still surviving perfectly preserved. Commissioned in Boston in 1797, the *Constitution* carried forty-four guns and a crew of four hundred and seventy-five. She served in the Tripolitan War between 1803 and 1805, and the peace treaty was signed in her cabin on 3 July, 1805. The *Constitution* was

114

Cane to celebrate Perry's victory on Lake Erie, inscribed: "We have met the enemy and they are ours." FLAYDERMAN COLLECTION

Group of commemorative and presentation canes made of wood from ships. Left to right: (1) from the frigate Constitution; (2) cane inscribed: "Part of Constitution presented by Com. S. T. Elliott to R. E. W. Earle, 1834"; (3) cane made from wood of HMS Victory; (4) cane from wood of Commodore Oliver Hazard Perry's flagship, the St. Lawrence. FLAYDERMAN COLLECTION

dubbed "Old Ironsides" after she defeated the *Guerrière* during the War of 1812. Although she is the flagship of the Commandant, First Naval District, "Old Ironsides" stays berthed in the Boston Naval Shipyard year-round as a tourist attraction and historical museum.

Commemoratives of the *Constitution* were made during the ship's long life. Then, when the keel was laid for rebuilding in 1927, small parts of the ship that were removed for restoration or replacement were made into souvenir items. Canes, paperweights, small boxes, are all suitably inscribed to identify the wood from "Old Ironsides." Of more historical importance than the later souvenirs are the two canes illustrated here, one dated 1824 and the other 1834. It has been observed that if all pieces of wood taken from the *Constitution* were put back together they would constitute enough lumber to build a fleet of frigates, but these may all be bona fide relics of historical significance. A sailing ship required constant replacement of its wood throughout its lifetime, and it is probable that the early souvenirs

Relic from the ship Constitution. FLAYDERMAN COLLECTION

This paperweight was probably sold to raise funds for the restoration of the Constitution. FLAYDERMAN COLLECTION

116

Ship's bell. FLAYDERMAN COLLECTION

"Sow's ears" were leaves that were dried, polished and painted at
Table Bay in Cape Town, South Africa, by natives. Sold to sailors
of incoming ships, these could be mailed home in an envelope.
FLAYDERMAN COLLECTION

Color prints of the familiar "Sailor's Return"
and "Sailor's Farewell,"
tinseled and decorated,
were cut out and the
fabric inserted in back
for clothing. FLAYDER-
MAN COLLECTION

"Sailor's valentine" in Barbados shellwork.
FLAYDERMAN COLLECTION

American sailor's embroidered jumper, made during the Civil War period. FLAYDERMAN COLLECTION

Left: Picture of an American ship embroidered in wool, probably in England. *Right:* A relic of early steamship days, this shell has engraved within the shield the words: "The Great Britain Steam Ship, 3500 tons." A portrait of Napoleon, Emperor of France, adorns the opposite side, along with design of acorns and oak leaves. Also the words: "The whole thing executed with a common pen knife." BOTH PHOTOS FLAYDERMAN COLLECTION

Figurehead from the ship *Bosphorus,* believed to have been built and owned in Sicily. Originally a brigantine, she was later lengthened to a three-master and called "Old Turk." VALHALLA MARITIME MUSEUM

Valentine made by a British sailor, cut from paper, then drawn and painted. Hearts enclose eight verses. This very rare original work is probably late eighteenth century.
FLAYDERMAN COLLECTION

Group of Chinese porcelain objects decorated for the American market. The large platter *(center bottom)* is a memorial of George Washington. The sauce plate in front of it is from George Washington's own service set ordered from China and decorated with the insignia of the Order of the Cincinnati, upheld by a figure of Fame.
SHELBURNE MUSEUM

Glass beaker with enameled naval scene, early nineteenth century. Made in England. FLAYDERMAN COLLECTION

Hand-painted jug for the British market depicting a compass surrounded by patriotic devices. FLAYDERMAN COLLECTION

Left: Unusual hand-painted plate with picture of sailor and lady. Verse reads: "O fair Brittania lovely dear, My vows shall always true remain, Let me kiss off that falling tear, We only part to meet again." "On board the Sunbeam." Late nineteenth Century. *Right:* Elsinore hand-painted bowl, decorated to order and carrying portrait of a ship. BOTH PHOTOS FLAYDERMAN COLLECTION

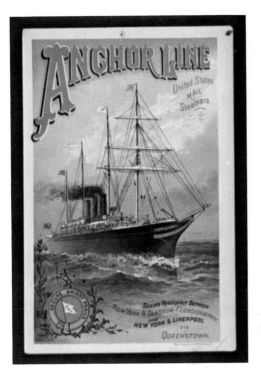

Anchor Line advertising card. FLAYDERMAN COLLECTION

"The Sperm Whale in a Flurry," a colorful nineteenth-century print. SHELBURNE MUSEUM

Presentation or commemorative goblet. Etched and gilded. "Bridport and Howe and heros like these. Shall make Briton's proud flag still exolt on the seas. JAB. Success to the *Leopard*." These goblets were made to celebrate a launching. FLAYDERMAN COLLECTION

Candlesticks made of timber taken from HMS *Brittania.* FLAYDERMAN COLLECTION

such as boxes and canes were made by ship's carpenters with leftover wood following needed repairs to the ship.

Relics of ships that played an important role in naval history have always been in demand by collectors. At first these were made as collectors' objects or presentation pieces, and most of them are small, decorative and usually not as expensive as some other categories of nautical antiques. A group of polished wood objects made from the beams, planks and other parts of historic ships makes a handsome display, and its associations are of interest to all naval and marine historians.

Objects that tell a story and are easily dated are always in favor with collectors. Awards of merit for individual or collective bravery on the high seas tell of heroic deeds and of the courage and perseverance of sailors of every nationality and station in coming to the aid of their fellows whenever the need arose. Even in times of peace, the life expectancy of a sailing man was shorter than that of his landbound brethren. Ships caught fire, struck reefs or broke up in storms with alarming frequency. Normal everyday duties of the seaman

Miniature barrel with self-explanatory plaque. FLAYDERMAN
COLLECTION

*Right and far right: Small
box in shape of a book, a
hand-carved relic of* HMS
Eurydice, *which foundered
off the Isle of Wight in
March, 1878.* FLAYDERMAN
COLLECTION

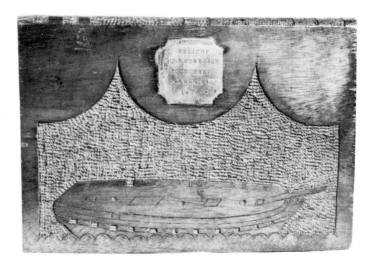

118

Patriotic bronze sculpture mounted on wood from the frigate Cumberland. FLAYDERMAN COLLECTION

were fraught with peril during the sailing-ship era and, surefooted though they were, many sailors fell from their ship's rigging to be lost overboard or fatally injured on the deck below.

Except in times of war, national origins have always been ignored when a ship is in distress and maritime history is rich in stories of acts of bravery on the part of entire crews or individual seamen in coming to the aid of a foundering ship.

When these lifesaving ventures involved a government ship or a person of station and means, they were usually rewarded. The awards came in many forms and depended upon the donor and the recipi-

Front and reverse of three British navy medals. Left: For service in the Orient in 1843. Center: For service in Canton during the Opium Wars. Right: For Arctic discoveries.
FLAYDERMAN COLLECTION

ent. Medals were the most common of all rewards for meritorious action at sea. Silver trophies can also be found, but these were not often given by governments to individuals. One such trophy, illustrated here, is typical of the gratitude expressed by the donor, whose life was saved in a shipwreck. The inscription reads:

> To JOHN BETHAN, ESQUIRE
> Captain of the Honorable Company's Marine
> One of His Majesty's Justice of the Peace
> for the Town of Madras and Marine Police Magistrate
> Who so eminently distinguished himself in the
> cause of humanity on the 24th of October, 1818,
> when the Ship *Success* was wrecked in a dreadful
> gale of wind near Madras.
> This cup is presented as a token of heartfelt
> regard by his friend, John Charles Parker,
> Whose life was saved with that of his infant son and
> two servants on that memorable occasion.

Silver and silver-gilt presentation cup for lifesaving feat of John Bethan of Madras in 1818. FLAY-DERMAN COLLECTION

This rifle with its elaborate silver inlay was the appropriate gift from the British government to the Arab hero who helped to rescue the crew of the brig Escape *in March 1858.* FLAYDER-MAN COLLECTION

The magnificent silver and silver-gilt presentation cup with a finial in the shape of a sailor leaning against an anchor is of historical and artistic importance. It serves as a memorial to the loss of the *Success* as well as a tribute to the man who was responsible for saving the lives of her passengers. It is probable that many other hands aided in the rescue, but the cup was presented to a person of some importance by another member of his class whom he was able to help.

Individual bravery on the part of sailors was usually rewarded with less ostentatious medals and presentation gifts. This is a vast and specialized field of collecting, and there is a variety of naval awards that have been presented by all seafaring nations of the world. Within the confines of this chapter, only a few such medals can be discussed or illustrated, but there is more specific literature for naval historians who pursue this aspect of the hobby.

Many of the medals given for brave deeds in the act of saving a life or lives at sea are as important in the history of art as they are in nautical history. Every country has had its own medallic designs, often made by important sculptors, and there are special categories of awards for each nation. Styles of medals often changed throughout history, but the materials used for them are usually bronze, silver or gold. One especially handsome medal, illustrated here, is a reward of merit for courage and perseverance presented by the Humane Society of the Refuge of Massachusetts to Alexander Burnett of the S. S. *Timor* for rescuing the officers and crew of the schooner *William and Richard* on 31 December, 1887. Other medals bear likenesses of naval heroes of the countries they represent, or national seals or symbols.

Telescopes and binoculars in presentation boxes were often given to sailors who performed an act of bravery and daring in saving lives

Bronze Reward of Merit for lifesaving from the Humane Society of Massachusetts, the first group to recognize the need for organized lifesaving efforts along the Atlantic coastline. FLAYDERMAN COLLECTION

Telescope awarded by the British government in 1865 to Alexander Leslie in recognition of his lifesaving feat. FLAYDERMAN COLLECTION

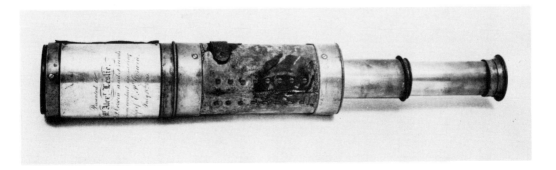

Binoculars presented by the British Government to Captain A. F. Thompson of the US brig Thomas Turrell *in acknowledgment of his humanity and kindness to the crew of the schooner* Cotnam *in 1868.* FLAYDERMAN COLLECTION

at sea, and these seem to have been the customary reward from the British government to American sailors helpful in rescuing the crews of British ships.

A pair of binoculars in a presentation box inscribed "Presented by the British Government to Captain A. F. Thompson of the U.S. brig "Thomas Turrell" in acknowledgement of his humanity and kindness to the crew of the schooner "Cotnam" of Windsor, N.S., whom he rescued from their sinking vessel on 25th Feby., 1868" is typical of the gracious "thank you" accorded the master of any ship involved in a lifesaving operation of the type described.

While the captain of a ship might have been rewarded with an elaborate pair of binoculars, the usual gift for a member of a crew was a telescope. These are inscribed in the manner of one illustrated here: "Life saving award from the British Government to an American sailor, 1862, Mr. Joseph Qualey." Although presentation telescopes are dated and suitably inscribed, there are usually fewer facts of the rescue given in the inscription. It would take lengthy research to attempt to trace the particular naval disaster in which seaman Qualey took part.

While most sailors were always willing to risk their lives to save others from the watery death that they also feared, there were many other men of historical importance who performed acts of bravery for their governments during service in the navy and suffered unusual hardships in carrying out their missions. These deeds did not go unrewarded, either. This is evident in the presentation objects that can be found today that record many of the remarkable missions undertaken by naval heroes.

William Edward Parry (1790–1855) joined the Royal Navy in 1804 and commanded three expeditions to Canada in search of a northwest passage to the Pacific between 1819 and 1825. On his first expedition he discovered the Parry Islands, which include Devon, Cornwallis and Melville, and penetrated to longitude 114 degrees West, a new record. Parry was the recipient of many awards from his government for his accomplishments. He was knighted in 1829 and made a rear admiral in 1852. After his first expedition, the City of Bath honored the explorer and presented him with the small box illustrated in this book.

The Parry presentation box is made of oak from his ship the *Hecla* and is decorated with molded gold mounts. The lid has a chased oval medallion in gold of a three-masted ship sailing in the lee of an iceberg, within a garland of oak leaves and acorns. The box is gold lined and inscribed inside the lid: "Presented to William Edward Parry, esq^r./ Commander in the Royal Navy/ by/ The Mayor, Aldermen & Common Council/ of the City of Bath/ As a token of their high sense of Importance/ of his late discoveries in the Polar Re-

A telescope in a presentation box such as this was usually given to any American sailor who saved the life of a British seaman. FLAYDERMAN COLLECTION

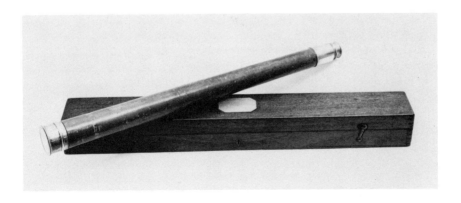

Medal and miniature portrait presented by Lord Nelson to
ship's surgeon at request of crew. Front and back of medal
with inscription and engraving. FLAYDERMAN COLLECTION

gions/ And the many eminent qualities displayed by him/ During
that perilous expedition."

On the front of the box is a gold plaque inscribed: "Made from
the oak of the Ship Hecla/ Commanded by Wm. Parry/ and presented With the Freedom of the City of Bath 24 March, 1821." This
presentation box is as important for the history it represents as it is
for the artistry in its design.

An extremely interesting presentation medal with strong British
naval associations includes a miniature portrait and was given by
Horatio Nelson to Arthur Ahmuty, M.D.E., Licentiate Royal College
of Surgeons, London, and Surgeon, Royal Navy. A rather lengthy
commendation is engraved on the medal:

> Sir
> The Officer's, Warrants and Petty
> Officers of his *Majesty's* Ship under *My Command*
> Having requested me to present you with this

medal as a mark of their appreciation of your conduct
I therefore beg your acceptance
I am Sir your hum. ser. Nelson
Egmont 20th April 1801

This medallion, dated a few months after Nelson had been pro-
moted Vice-Admiral of the Blue, was probably not personally pre-

*Pocket compass/sundial, a presentation piece from the
Franco-Indian War period. Brass with paper label pasted
inside cover. Above left: Lid with date 1762 and inscription
"Havana." Above right: Bottom. Below: Compass sundial
open and compass paper in lid.* FLAYDERMAN COLLECTION

sented by the naval hero, since he was engaged in the Battle of Copenhagen at the time. However, it is one of the few Nelson-related relics that survive from the hero's lifetime. Most Nelson-related collectibles are memorials or commemoratives made after he met his death at Trafalgar.

During England's long naval history, engravers of silver and gold medals were kept busy engraving accolades to recipients of government awards who had aided in lifesaving maneuvers in various parts of the world. An unusual gift of the British government, typical of this show of gratitude, is the rifle illustrated here. From the inscription on the stock it is obvious that if the brig *Escape* did not survive a shipwreck, its crew did, due to the kindness of Sheik Mohamed Ben Boudera.

Watches, chronometers and pocket compasses were other gifts that, suitably inscribed, became thank-you tokens for service beyond the call of duty or as tokens of esteem from one seaman to another. The pocket compass/sundial illustrated here is a relic of the French-Indian War period and is inscribed, "Havana 1762/ Presented to Captain Wellock, H.B.M.S. Pembroke/ By his confident Capt. Arbuthnot, H.B.M.S. Orford." The compass is brass and has a paper compass rose pasted on the inside lid.

A watch with presentation case was also given for meritorious serv-

Presentation watch from the Prince of Wales to a member of the Royal Navy. FLAYDERMAN COLLECTION

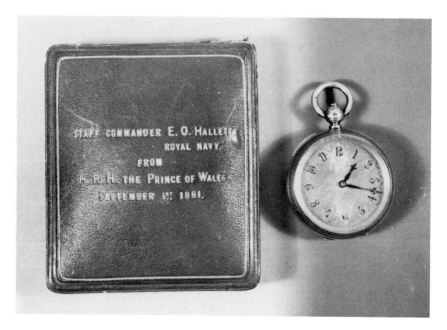

Condiment set with nautical motifs, a presentation from the United States Navy to Rear-Admiral Francis H. Gregory "for valuable services rendered to his country, 1864." FLAY-DERMAN COLLECTION

Brass box, British, with engraving of HMS
Warrior, *presented to George Greatcroft
from his son-in-law, Tom Heath, in 1865.*
FLAYDERMAN COLLECTION

Nelson medal commemorating the victory of Trafalgar.
FLAYDERMAN COLLECTION

*Medal, "Earl St. Vincent's Testimony of Approbation,"
dated 1800.* FLAYDERMAN COLLECTION

ice to Staff Commander E. O. Hallett, R.N., from the Prince
of Wales, on 1 September, 1881. Another silver-cased watch has
nautical motifs around the edge and was probably a presentation
piece also.

*Nelson award medal presented by the British government
to John McDonald of "Belleisle."* FLAYDERMAN COLLECTION

French maritime award presented to an American, Captain Nichols, in 1874. FLAYDERMAN COLLECTION

A presentation box with more personal associations along with its nautical design is a small brass box with a hinged lid. The lid has an engraving of a ship and the inscription, "HMS Warrior/ Presented to Geo. Greatcroft/ By his Son-in-law/ 1865/ Tom Heath."

These are only a few of the presentation and award objects that can be found with nautical associations. Shipwrecks were so common in the days of sailing ships that the history of many of these naval disasters has gone unrecorded, and were it not for the presentation boxes, medals, watches and other gifts that were made and that still exist, the identity of many a brave and selfless hero would have been lost to history.

11

SHIP FURNITURE, CHESTS AND BOXES

On board a sailing vessel, the seamen lived in communal closeness and had room for little more than a sea chest or duffel bag. On most merchant ships the men had to provide their own bedding and eating utensils, and were fortunate if they had a place to hang their oilskins. Senior officers usually had their own cabins, while petty officers shared a cabin that was generally very small, damp and stuffy. The captain's quarters alone had some degree of spaciousness but in a merchant vessel it was often the case that their furnishing was the responsibility of the master himself. All such furniture had to be easily portable and even pieces of case furniture for ships in the domestic styles of the eighteenth and nineteenth centuries which have come to light often have handles by which they can be lifted. In some instances, larger pieces of furniture, such as a desk, would be made in two parts that would fold into box-shaped structures.

The degree of luxury to be found in the master's quarters depended upon the size of his ship and the purpose for which it was built. Flagships of naval fleets were often luxuriously outfitted to accommodate the visits of important personages. An interior view of the admiral's quarters aboard H.M.S. *Victory* indicates that the cabins and saloon were luxuriously furnished with carpeting, draperies, a desk and upholstered chairs and sofas.

The master of a merchant vessel lived in less spacious surroundings, though by comparison with the cramped and draughty quarters of his crew and petty officers, it was relative comfort. It was not

Seaman's chest, of camphorwood with brass hardware, made in Singapore in the mid-1800s. Single-lock and double-lock chests in a variety of sizes were made. AUTHOR'S COLLECTION

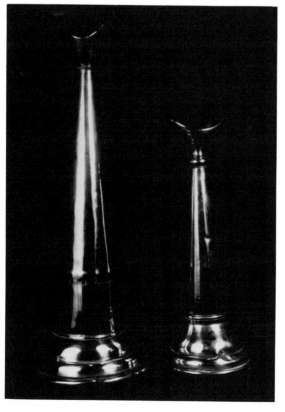

Speaking trumpets, used for ship-to-ship communication at sea, were the property of the captains. FLAYDERMAN COLLECTION

Left: Mast alarm, obviously hand-made and primitive, possibly used to announce mealtimes. When handle is turned, the alarm makes a loud clacking sound. FLAYDERMAN COLLECTION *Right: This later and more carefully made mast alarm makes a similarly effective sound when the handle is turned.* FLAYDERMAN COLLECTION

unusual for the master's family to accompany him on voyages, and it is probable that many masters' salons were decorated with the aid of a "woman's touch."

A desk of ample size was a necessity for the officers responsible for keeping accurate records and logs, and letter writing was a regular task for men away from home for years at a time. Ship's desks range from full-size drop-front desks that become two sea chests when folded for transporting, to compact writing boxes that store conveniently when not in use.

When a writing desk or box can be found with definite naval or marine associations, it becomes a bonus for collectors. Writing compendiums and boxes were in common use during the eighteenth and nineteenth centuries, and similar boxes were used by military as well as naval men. They were also popular items among the civilian population as traveling desks. It is therefore difficult to distinguish

Sea captain's writing desk, a presentation piece from a Dutch
admirer. Below: Elaborate desk for captain's quarters, divided into two sections to facilitate carrying on and off a
ship. BOTH PHOTOS: FLAYDERMAN COLLECTION

among the plain wood writing boxes with brass or silver hardware, but there are a few that can be found with definite nautical associations. A writing box such as the one illustrated here has indisputable importance as a marine antique. The brass plate on its lid is inscribed: "Remembrance to Capt. Wm. H. Hunt of the American Barque Apollo from his friend Van den Burgh fils, Ship broker, Antwerp."

Of a more luxurious nature is the drop-front desk with brass hardware. Although it is similar to domestic desks of the early nineteenth century, concessions on the part of the cabinetmaker to marine use are evident in the recessed hardware on the fronts of the drawers and the carrying handles on the sides. The desk divides into two sections, making it easier to move on or off the ship.

The unusual piece of ship's furniture illustrated here is an indication that its owner did not lack for the luxuries of indoor plumbing while traveling. It is a clever combination desk-lavatory. The sloped

Handy slanted writing top conceals the sink of this "cabin convenience." Other earthenware accessories are stored in compartments below. FLAYDERMAN COLLECTION

Chart box from the Volant *in painted wood grain.* FLAY-
DERMAN COLLECTION

writing surface lifts up to reveal a decorated earthenware sink, and
the presence of two brass spigots indicates that the master of the ship
who owned this convenience was supplied with hot water. While his
crew washed themselves and their clothes in tin basins on deck, the
privilege of rank was seldom questioned in the despotic way of a
ship's life. Other articles necessary to indoor comfort were stored
within this handy cabin furniture. This traveling water closet is a
rare piece of Victoriana. Disguised as a desk, it could be carried
anywhere.

Chests of many sizes and styles were carried aboard ship for stor-
age. Charts were vital to the safety and well-being of all ships, and
were kept in wooden chests for protection. Collectors search for chart
chests that are painted or imprinted with the name of a ship, such as
the painted grain chest illustrated here from the bark *Volant.*

Sailors often constructed their own sea chests. The early ones were
sometimes built by the ship's carpenter out of teak if the sailor could
afford it. The sea chest was the only furniture to be found in crew's
quarters, and it was both worktable and seat for its owner. Usually

left unpainted on the outside, sailor's chests were sometimes embellished with paintings of a ship inside the lid and usually the name or initials of its owner. A chest owned by a sailor was of great importance to him. Besides serving as furniture, it stored all of his possessions. His clothing, tools, patching and mending material and all that he made or purchased on his voyage had to fit inside the wooden box.

Great care was taken in constructing a sea chest so that it would last for many years. The early chests had sloping sides to give some stability in rough weather and often a small interior compartment was installed on one side to keep within reach the small impedimenta needed for mending and sailmaking. The early sea chests were usually only three feet in length since space was valuable in the crew's cramped quarters.

While the outside of a sea chest was quite plain, the interior compartment lid was often intricately carved. Many sailors made handsome carved beckets with elaborate woven rope handles embellished with fancy knots. The ability to work with rope was a necessity for every seafarer, and this art, as expressed in chest handles, was always

Left: This handsome becket (handle for a seaman's chest) is a fine example of sailor's carving and fancy rope work. FLAYDERMAN COLLECTION *Right: Carved beckets from seaman's chest.* FLAYDERMAN COLLECTION

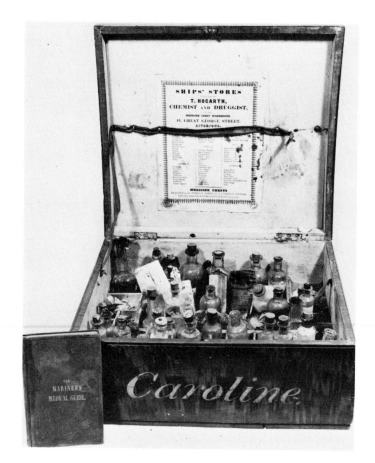

an individual expression of the pride a sailor took in this special talent and skill.

Since it was intended to be sat upon, the lid of the sailor's chest was often covered with canvas and sometimes edged with rope-work fringe. This sort of painted sailor's chest, used in the eighteenth and early nineteenth centuries, seems to have been more common among the Dutch and Germans, but decorated chests have been found that can be attributed to sailors of other nationalities. During the nineteenth century, crews of merchant sailing ships were international in nature, and sailors were inspired to try any craft that could be practiced aboard ship.

Clipper-ship traders were frequently supplied with handsome camphorwood chests that could be purchased in Singapore. These are less crude than the sailor-made chests and have brass fittings and single or double locks. Handles on the sides made for convenient transporting, and the thick, solid, fragrant wood probably appealed to seamen who were used to less pleasant odors. These decorative, practical chests are in demand now by decorators and collectors, and can sometimes be found with the name of the maker stamped inside the lid. These stamps are usually in English and Chinese, attesting to the fact that incoming ships provided lucrative trade for merchants in ports all over the world.

The sailor who was, in the words of W. S. Gilbert, "hardly ever sick at sea," was indeed fortunate, since there was hardly ever anyone on board capable of treating any type of serious malady. Doctors were never carried except on passenger ships, and even then they were frequently drunks or disenchanted with medical practice to the point where they could manage to overlook any but the most obvious and easily treatable symptoms.

On British ships masters were required to carry a medicine chest as part of their supplies, and it is probable that by the start of the nineteenth century this was common practice on board most ships. The "doctor's box" was fitted with numerous bottles and jars filled with powders and potions, plus a copy of *The Ship Master's Medical Guide* or *The Mariner's Medical Guide*. The books make interesting reading today, but it is obvious from the descriptions of how to treat such diverse complaints as "nettle rash," "locked jaw," "vermin,"

Water keg from an American whaling ship, first half of the nineteenth century.
SUFFOLK COUNTY WHALING MUSEUM

141

Rum kegs with earthenware labels were probably returned to the vendor on return to port. FLAYDERMAN COLLECTION

"scurvy" or "inflammation of the brain" that an experienced seaman would have to be dying in his hammock before he would present himself to the master for treatment.

Small as well as serious injuries were commonplace aboard sailing ships, and wounds were dressed and bandaged by the captain or a ship's officer. In cases of serious illness—and when it was possible—a ship put into the nearest port and left the patient to receive medical attention and find his own way home when he had recovered. He sometimes shipped on another vessel or was picked up by his own on its return voyage. Risk to life and limb was so commonplace for the sailor that serious injury, illness and death are seldom noted in many logs and journals. Deaths and subsequent burials at sea were recorded by a coffin-shaped stamp in some logs.

Doctor's boxes of special interest to collectors are those engraved or painted with the name of a ship or the master to whom the box belonged. These are historically associated nautical times. The boxes were frequently made of mahogany with brass hardware. Many of them still hold a fascinating array of colorful medications. There are

142

some medical boxes still to be found that contain a wealth of early blown bottles plus the medical-practice-made-easy books from which the do-it-yourself doctors made the diagnoses and found the suitable cures. Some ship's doctor's boxes have secret compartments which we can only assume were meant to hide drugs that might become desirable to a man confined to a ship for many months.

All chests and boxes with nautical associations are of interest to collectors, from the iron-bound strongboxes with their intricate locks to the heavy lockers used aboard later naval vessels. When there is evidence of a sailor's handwork or a definite nautical association, all ship's furniture is of interest to the collector.

12
LIGHTING DEVICES

The most decorative and certainly, to the collector of nautical antiques, the most desirable of all ship lighting devices would be a stern lantern from a seventeenth- or early eighteenth-century English, Spanish, Dutch or French ship. Few of these have survived, and these elaborate lanterns can only be seen today in engravings and paintings or on models of these heavily decorated ships.

The British standardized ship lantern shapes around 1715 and thereafter all stern lanterns were hexagonal, with an occasional octagonal variant. These lamps had glass panels, usually four or six to a side, and a group of three lanterns was used high up on the stern. One lamp dominated the center stern, and the remaining two were placed one on either side.

Providing lighting inside or outside a ship required extreme care in design. The danger of fire aboard vessels made entirely of wood was always great, and lanterns that protected the flame from drafts came into early use afloat. Moreover, it was necessary that a lamp could be fixed in some manner, either by hanging it on a bracket or attaching it to the wall by a hook. This lessened the danger of a lamp falling to the deck in rough weather. Frequently lanterns were made so that they could convert from a hanging fixture to a carrying light.

Candles and lanterns were used with great caution aboard the old sailing vessels and designs of early lanterns attest to the fact that the amount of light one would provide was less important than that the flame be enclosed and protected. A brass lantern from a British ship, dating around 1720, has a straight cylindrical body fitted with glass panels and covered with wire guards. It is, of course, fitted for a candle, and the conical top is hinged. It could be carried around by its handle or hung from a bracket or peg when used in a cabin.

British ship's lamps of a later period, around 1760, are better adapted for hanging on the wall. They have a flat back and a three-sided front with glass panels. These also could be converted to hand lanterns. They were made of brass and fitted to burn whale oil.

The American ship's cabin lantern illustrated here, circa 1750, is made of wood, has a rope handle and is two feet high. The great size of this light attests to the fact that it is candle-burning, and adequate space had to be allowed so that the flame would not ignite the wooden case. The lantern is hexagonal, and the top and one side panel are hinged.

Passengers on the *Mayflower* brought with them the primitive loose-wick lamps that had been in use for centuries and it was not until the eighteenth century that improvement in lighting devices for ship or shore came about. It is probable that all of these improvements, including the channeled wick lamp, were used aboard ships as

American cabin lantern, 24 inches in height and used with candles. Made circa 1750. PEABODY MUSEUM

145

Brass ship's lamps. Center lantern, circa 1720, is one of earliest types of marine lamps used on British ships. Left and right are a pair of English ship's lamps, circa 1760, fitted for whale oil.

soon as they became used domestically, and gradually replaced the more expensive and dangerous open candle. The availability of whale oil led to the use of the enclosed-wick lamp, and a variety of whale-oil lamps was used on ships throughout the nineteenth century. The elaborateness of the lamp forms depended upon the type of ship for which they were intended.

Perforated tin lanterns, of the type called "Paul Revere," were a fairly safe but rather ineffectual means of providing light on ships. More intense light was provided by the tin, brass or sheet-copper lanterns with glass-paneled sides. Lamps were designed for special purposes, and binnacles as well as compass boxes frequently were made with attached whale-oil lamps.

Port and starboard lanterns, fitted with red or green corrugated glass lenses, have always been essential to safe navigation. A large variety of shapes and sizes in whale-oil lanterns that have definite ship associations can be found, but it is sometimes difficult to differentiate between those made for shore use and the lighting devices especially designed for ships. The same degree of caution was necessary when flame was to be used around a farm, and it is probable that lanterns made for general outdoor use were also purchased for ships. It can also be assumed that oil-burning lamps as well as candles continued to be used on ships until the days of sail were over.

146

In the area of lighting devices, the collector interested only in nautical items should search for lanterns with ship provenance. Those lamps made as attachments to binnacles or compass boxes are desirable collectors' items. Any whale-oil lamp is, of course, sea-related. Were it not for the enormous quantities of oil brought back by lengthy whaling expeditions, illumination would have been available throughout the nineteenth century only to those who could afford expensive candles.

One type of lighting device designed only for ship use is the gimbal lamp. This was an enclosed-wick light attached to a metal ring that surrounded the reservoir of oil. When a ship pitched or rolled, the lamp maintained a horizontal position and kept the oil from spilling or the flame from reaching flammable material. Com-

Left: This pierced tin lantern, from an American whaling ship, did not give much light but was relatively safe. SUFFOLK COUNTY WHALING MUSEUM *Right: A great buoy lantern, of brass and glass, with extra large reservoir for whale oil to avoid refilling.* FLAYDERMAN COLLECTION

Left: A ship's light which could be carried or hung on the wall. From an American whaling ship. SUFFOLK COUNTY WHALING MUSEUM *Above: This gimbal lamp could be used as a table light, carried, or hung on a nail.* SUFFOLK COUNTY WHALING MUSEUM

Left: Double-wick brass gimbal lamp, nineteenth century. FLAYDERMAN COLLECTION *Right: Binnacle containing an American-made compass illuminated by the whale-oil lantern attached.* SUFFOLK COUNTY MUSEUM

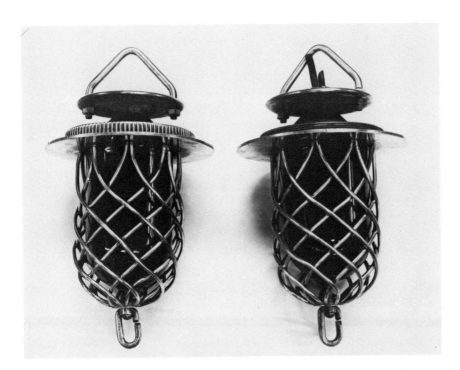

Port and starboard side of lights, brass and glass, as used in small craft at the turn of the century. FLAYDERMAN COLLECTION

passes were mounted in a similar manner.

There were other ingenious types of lighting devices designed for ship use. Many had large-size reservoirs so that they did not require frequent filling. This was particularly important when the light was oversize or in a place that was difficult to reach.

Ship lights of the late nineteenth century vary in type and style and depend upon the purpose for which they were made. Elaborate quarters on a passenger ship used lighting fixtures as elegant as one could find in any public building on land, while the whaling ships and trading ships continued to be fitted with plainer lighting devices.

13

SEAPORT SOUVENIRS AND SAILORS' CRAFTS

Like his counterpart in the whaling ship, the merchant seaman who had a family at home did not often come back empty-handed from a lengthy sea voyage. If he had a special talent and liking for handwork, he made a gift or two from materials he could find on the ship. If not, there were souvenirs in many of the world's ports made to fit the meager pocketbook of the lowly sailor. More expensive souvenir items were available for the ship's officers. Any token, usually decorated with a remembrance of an exotic foreign country and a ship, would convince a faithful wife or sweetheart that her sailor had been thinking of her.

As opposed to the whaling man who, when there were no whales to kill, had to find methods of killing time instead, the merchant seaman was often on an undermanned ship where he worked every minute he was on duty and caught whatever sleep he could between four-hour watches. This is the reason that there is so little handwork made by the merchant seaman and so much left by the whalers. The merchant seaman did not especially search for occupational therapy on his busy voyages and, like the crews of naval vessels who were also kept fully occupied, he fell an easy victim to purveyors of souvenir items at foreign ports.

In many marine antiques collections there are framed shell pictures that have become known as "sailors' valentines." These are usually two octagonal wooden frames, hinged on one side and with a catch on the other so that they close into boxes. The frames have

Above: Wood cane made by a sailor and carved with hand and anchor "tattoo" motif. FLAYDERMAN COLLECTION

Nautical and American patriotic symbols decorate this carved box. FLAYDERMAN COLLECTION

Carved box with ship and American patriotic designs. FLAYDERMAN COLLECTION

glass fronts. Within them are shells in a variety of colors arranged in pleasing symmetrical designs. Messages such as "A Gift," "Home Sweet Home," "Home Again," "With Love" or "Truly Thine" are laid out in shells in the centers of these pictures. These "sailors' valentines," until recently thought to have been another of the sailor's crafts, were produced as souvenir items in the West Indies and are made up of the great variety of colorful miniature seashells indigenous to that area of the world.

The decoration used in the Barbados framed shell pictures vary only slightly. Geometric and floral designs are the most common. Heart motifs are also quite usual, and it is from these and the sentiments spelled out in tiny shells that the pictures get their name.

The frames, made of Spanish cedar, are from twelve to sixteen inches in diameter. These "sailors' valentines" are carefully made and have stood up well through the years, attesting to the fact that they were put together with great care and patience. A few have been found with the labels of the West Indian merchant who sold them. Souvenir gifts such as these made welcome additions to overstuffed Victorian parlors in the nineteenth century.

Of an entirely different nature is the *true* sailor's valentine illustrated in this book. Probably no more pleasing love token has ever been produced by hand with just a piece of paper, a sharp cutting tool, some paint and pen and ink. This valentine is entirely original and altogether charming. It is obvious that the British sailor who made it had a wife and child very much in his thoughts. The center motif is a picture of his ship under full sail and from this carefully drawn and painted vignette emanate eight hearts divided by laurel sprays. Surrounding these is a border of family groups of father, mother and child, which alternate with urns of flowers. Around this complicated cutout is a border of cross-hatching and corner designs of birds and flowers.

Within each of the eight hearts is a valentine verse, each one numbered so that they can be read in sequence. As is true of most eighteenth-century British sailors, the spelling is less strong than the sentiment. One of the verses reads:

> But when that you those lines do see
> Bestow your love on none but me
> So let our harts no more be twine
> But be my loving Valentine.

That this fragile bit of paper has lasted through the years is evidence that it was appreciated by its recipient. It was framed, and therefore protected from damage and loss early in its history.

Sailors did make objects from shells to bring home as gifts, but these were usually simple box-shaped wood frames with shells and sentiment glued into them. The variety and coloring of the shells are not as exotic as the Barbados shell pictures. Toward the middle of the nineteenth century, shell picture frames were made by sailors to hold the daguerreotype pictures they carried in their seabags or chests. These frames were usually made of putty with the seashells pushed into it.

Examples of fancy rope work are also found on occasion. Small mats or cane heads were made of rope. The sailor prided himself on his ability to work with rope and to make complicated knots. Some-

Left: Shellwork picture frame made by a sailor in the mid-1800s. FLAYDERMAN COLLECTION *Right: Bottle covered with fancy rope work and painted marine blue. Decorative knotting was a typical sailor's art.* FLAYDERMAN COLLECTION

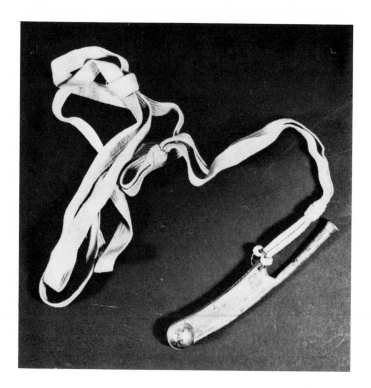

Bosun's whistles can often be found with knotwork lanyards made by sailors.
FLAYDERMAN COLLECTION

times ordinary objects easily found aboard ship were covered or embellished with rope. One example is the bottle illustrated here. It has a hand-knotted rope covering and a fancywork tassel, and is painted a bright marine blue. The sailor of a merchant ship who might be moved in an odd moment to produce a gift to take home had to make do with the tools and materials on shipboard, and there was no shortage of bottles or rope.

If the creative sailor had to devise his own method of making "a silk purse out of a sow's ear," there were natives of Cape Town in South Africa who made souvenir "sow's ears" out of leaves. From a plant leaf in their area, the ingenious souvenir makers of Table Bay treated these leaves so that they resembled silk. The leaves had a fuzzy outer layer that was cleaned off. Then the surface was painted with pictures of ships that were in the harbor or messages embellished with flags and other patriotic motifs. The pale pink color of the leaf and its "hairy" outer edge do resemble the ear of a sow, and the colorful little souvenirs could be tucked into a letter. One journal-keeping sailor described the process used to clean the leaves and said, "It was frequently the case the remainder of this leaf is reserved FANCY for fine original painting as you will see."

A sailor adept at wood carving had many opportunities to purchase exotic wood in the ports he visited, and it was not unusual for a fancy box to be made and carved to be brought back as a gift. It is probable from the exceptional quality of many of the carved boxes that exist today that a large proportion of them were made by the "chippie" or ship's carpenter. Carved wood canes have also been found with definite nautical associations and motifs, and many of these are probably also the work of the experienced "chippie."

If we deduct the work of the prolific whaling man, examples of the seaman's art are scarce and difficult to find. Only when a sailor was faced with hours of leisure time aboard ship was there any great abundance of a particular type of handcrafted objects made on shipboard. This makes the scattered examples of the seaman's art more valuable to the collector. The merchant seaman who stood four-hour

Left: The strange mermaid carved into this small plank of wood was probably the work of a sailor. HEART AND STAR ANTIQUES *Right: Wood carving reminiscent of many sea stories and pirate adventures. The wooden leg belonged to a nineteenth-century sailor.* FLAYDERMAN COLLECTION

Copper and silver box, possibly sailor-made, early eighteenth century. Engraved on the lid: "Britons bold shall rule the Main, In spite of Holland, France or Spain." FLAYDERMAN COLLECTION

watches, mended sails and scraped and painted the ship in addition to many other duties would have to be highly disciplined to begin and finish any complicated project not required of him. Journals were kept and many were illustrated and artistically embellished, but few other constructive pastimes were indulged in or needed.

In some ports of the world there were artists who earned their livelihood by painting pictures of incoming ships on commission from their captains or other officers. While paintings and prints of ships are outside the scope of this book, it is important for the collector to know that artists who worked in media other than paint also earned their living making personalized souvenirs for seafarers. Some painted pictures of ships on pottery and porcelain. Others made skillful renderings of ships in wool embroidery (crewel work). Little is known of the origin of this work.

The making of woolen ship paintings seems to have been primarily a British skill. Most of the work of this type that exists today was probably done to order by professional needleworkers, just as the ship paintings were. Seamen who were especially adept at needlework also pursued this art form aboard ship. Many of the existing woolen ship paintings exhibit a high degree of knowledge of the art of tapestry design. The reason the embroidered pictures of ships can be referred to as "paintings" is that the stitches were used in a manner similar to the artist's brush stroke. Long or short, vertical or horizontal stitchery was used to give movement to waves and sails. Many of the wool paintings that we find today show evidence of a high degree of skill on the part of the makers. Unfortunately, few of them can be identified as to who made them and where.

Of special interest are the two wool pictures illustrated in this book that are portraits of whaling ships. Stitch direction gives

Wool painting of an American whaling ship. A blanket of blubber is being hauled aboard. FLAYDERMAN COLLECTION

Seabag of American sailor, embroidered with a picture of his ship and patriotic symbols. FLAYDERMAN COLLECTION

movement to the choppy seas and realism to the rigging. On one, the ship is shown under full sail, while in the other a sperm whale lies alongside the ship and a blanket of blubber is being hauled aboard.

Sailors on board British naval vessels were given time to work on embroideries if they were so disposed. During at least part of the nineteenth century, time was set aside on shipboard—called the "make and mend" period—during which the sailors were supposed to repair their clothing. While it is probable that this time was utilized more as a rest period than a sewing bee, there is evidence that at least some of the British wool embroidery made by sailors was produced during this time.

It was customary for sailors of the American Navy to embellish

158

their uniforms in some way in the nineteenth century. Naval regulations applying to uniforms were nonexistent until 1841, but even after that time sailors' blouses were sometimes embroidered with brightly colored patriotic or personalized designs. Probably these fancywork jumpers were worn only on shore leave, and they are rarely found today. The handsome jumper illustrated in this book is from the Civil War period. Embroidered on it is the name of the sailor's ship, "U.S. Steamer Richmond."

Seabags were another favorite place for the sailor to embroider his name and a picture of his ship. Often he used other patriotic devices such as the flag and stars or the American eagle. Further handwork of the sailor is evident in the fancy knots that he tied in his seabag rope. Sailors' jumpers being the impractical garment that they were, many sailors made purses to wear on shoulder straps under their jumpers. Some of these were made of leather; others were of cloth decorated with embroidery.

Just as whalebone was used as a medium for a form of art that could be picked up at any time and worked on at intervals, so embroidery was also a kind of busywork that could be put down at a moment's notice and continued later on. These were the types of craft in which the sailor could indulge. An unfinished embroidery or a whale's tooth could be tucked into a sea chest or seabag and taken out to be worked on whenever time allowed.

Of all sailors' embroidery, wool paintings have lasted in better condition than most other articles. They were usually framed and therefore protected from insects and dirt. All early embroidery with nautical motifs, whether done by the sailors themselves or executed by port artists, deserves recognition as worthwhile ship portraiture or personal artistic expression of the sailors. There is little doubt that many sailing men were quite capable of doing very complicated stitchery and the few examples of nineteenth-century embroidery that have come down to us are as deserving of attention as scrimshaw or the work of any port artist.

14

MARINE-RELATED CERAMICS

The vast fortunes made in the early days of trade with China are legendary, and the art objects that were carried across the oceans from the mid-seventeenth century to the nineteenth century went through many changes of style as taste in the West began to dictate design and decoration. The skilled craftsmen and artists of Canton provided merchants with articles made for Western taste and to specifications that would satisfy the foreign market.

In the second half of the eighteenth century, Dutch tradesmen employed draftsmen in China to decorate porcelain with Western figures and designs that would appeal to customers at home. It also became customary for shipowners and officers to order plates and punch bowls with paintings of their ships. These porcelain objects were all made to order, and the designs were painted while the ships lay in harbor at Canton. One of the earliest examples of this type of decorated Chinese porcelain is inscribed in Dutch, "Christopher Schooneman, Chief mate of the ship Vryburg, in the roads off Whampoo in China in the year 1736."

The Dutch also imported blank ceramicware and decorated it in their own country with familiar scenes and designs that would appeal to national pride. A plate made in China and decorated in Europe with a Dutch ship and the arms of Zeeland is in the British Museum in London. Dated 1700, it is the earliest known example of this type of work.

The fine small ships of the Dutch East India Company were responsible in the seventeenth century for the bulk of the world's carrying trade, and four fifths of all the merchant ships on the seas were owned by them. Any documented pottery or porcelain decorated with a portrait of one of these vessels with three masts, a bowsprit, topgallant sails on the fore and main masts and lofty stern would be a find for any collector of marine-related pottery and porcelain. However, seventeenth-century ceramics of any sort are rarely discovered outside of museums today, and collectors search for later documented nautically decorated pottery and porcelain.

"The United Company of Merchant Venturers of England Trading to the East Indies," more generally known as the East India Company, carried on an exclusive trade with India in the two centuries following 1600. A great many relics of the East India Company exist for collectors. In the area of ceramics decorated with marine motifs, there are many that have found their way into the great national and private collections in England and the United States.

British trade with China began later than the Dutch. It was not until 1715 that a "factory" was opened by the East India Company at Canton. Trade increased so rapidly following that earliest establishment of facilities that the East India Company probably did more business in the eighteenth and nineteenth centuries than all other trading nations combined. As quickly as the shipyards at Blackwall could turn out new merchantmen, the craftsmen of China manufactured merchandise for Western taste to fill them. Most certainly, the major product brought over on these ships was tea, but the cups, saucers, plates and pots needed for serving the drink were also imported in vast quantities.

The British sea captains were no less proud of their ships than the Dutch, and there exist today many plates, mugs and punch bowls with paintings of these East Indiamen. Some of the pieces of Chinese porcelain included in their decorations patriotic sentiments that would appeal to British sea captains or their friends at home. The hongs in Canton were also used as motifs as remembrances of a voyage, and bowls and other pieces of ceramics decorated in this manner show the buildings in the famous compound with the flags of the trading nations flying above them. They also show a variety of ships at anchor waiting to be loaded with the precious goods from the Orient that would bring high prices and great fortunes to the Crown, the owners and the masters of the ships. (Captains of the East India Company were allowed a small portion of the cargo area in their

Punch bowl with painting of a British ship on the front and the words "Pitt and Liberty" inscribed on the inside bottom.
MATTATUCK MUSEUM

ships for transporting goods that could bring them private profits.)
One example of Cantonese porcelain of British historical importance is the *famille rose* punch bowl illustrated here, decorated with

a British ship of the line. The phrase "Pitt and Liberty" is inscribed on the interior bottom of the bowl. This relic of the Napoleonic War period can easily be dated to the period prior to the disbandment of the East India Company. The early nineteenth century was the great era of this famous trading and ship-owning company, and to serve in one of its ships was equivalent in prestige to serving in the Royal Navy. During this period captains of the handsome vessels of the trading fleet were in constant danger of encountering French ships. Thus all carried, besides their precious cargoes, a full complement of guns and ammunition in the event that their journey to the East and back might be interrupted by an engagement with the enemy.

The East India Company monopolized eastern trade for two hundred years until, in 1814, the trade with India was thrown open to all merchants who could provide ships of more than three hundred and fifty tons. However, the company still reserved trade with China for itself, and continued until 1833 when the last of its exclusive rights was withdrawn.

Pottery and porcelain made and decorated in China with nautical motifs are in high demand and short supply today. These became the prototypes for pottery decoration in Great Britain in the late eighteenth century and throughout the nineteenth century. British potters were astute enough to realize that nautical motifs were desirable to the men responsible for sailing the ships that would carry their goods throughout the world. In addition, at the close of the Revolutionary War it was important to the British pottery industry that they capture as much of the American market as possible. One way to do this was to decorate their earthenware with patriotic or political motifs that would appeal to the chauvinism of a new republic.

The previously established tradition of decorating a jug, plate, mug or punch bowl with patriotic devices was borrowed from the Chinese by the British potters. Objects were made and decorated with designs that had meaning for the countries for which they were intended. Since one eighth of all workingmen in England were engaged in some sea-related work, it is obvious that British ships and sailors would be used in pottery decoration as soon as the ceramics industry became established in that country. The British potters also were aware of the lucrative market available to them in America. During the period following the Revolution, America, too, was a country whose commerce was almost entirely oriented toward the sea. It was well understood by British pottery decorators that ship

163

and sea motifs would be popular with Americans.

British potters were aware that the United States was no longer a captive market for British goods and that they were competing with the Chinese for the ceramics trade. The shipbuilders of New York and New England were well established by the time the New England merchants could reach out for their own share of the lucrative Far Eastern trade. Moreover, there were many members of the British pottery industry who were in sympathy with the American cause in the war, and many pieces of ceramics were made that reflect that feeling. Josiah Wedgwood was one potter who realized the great potential for trade with America, and he made portrait medallions of American patriots. Later, his company was to produce portraits of American naval heroes as well.

The earliest British ceramics made in some quantity and decorated with nautical motifs expressly for American customers are the punch bowls, jugs and mugs printed in Liverpool with pictures of ships in

THE ENTERPRIZE AND BOXER.

"The True Blooded Yan-kee" on a Liverpool jug, with pink luster band on rim. Made for the American market. MATTATUCK MUSEUM

"Commodore MacDonough's Victory," an American commemorative plate of white earthenware printed in deep blue. Made in England. MATTATUCK MUSEUM

166

"Cape Coast Castle on the Gold Coast of Africa," an Enoch Wood plate printed in dark blue for the American market, circa 1830. MATTATUCK MUSEUM

Liverpool harbor, or sailing the high seas. American sea captains at Liverpool ordered these printed wares for their own use or as gifts. Others were brought back in quantity for sale in the United States' seaport towns.

That so many Liverpool creamware ceramics should have been produced with American marine and naval designs is due to a fortuitous combination of circumstances. The process for printing decorations on china was discovered by a Liverpool printer, John Sadler, who opened an establishment at 14 Harrington Street in 1748. He later took Guy Green as a partner, and the firm continued in business until 1799. Sadler's discovery made it possible for ceramics to be decorated uniformly and cheaply. He did work for Liverpool pottery firms as well as for the many Staffordshire potters who sent their undecorated wares to the seaport city to be decorated, packed and shipped out. Some of the printed ware was sold with only the plain printed designs, while many others were overpainted with bright colors. This painting was not of the highest order and required only

Late eighteenth-century Staffordshire figure groups, the
"Sailor's Farewell" and the "Sailor's Return." Below: Two
nautical and naval mugs, both Nelson commemoratives,
made and printed for the British market. FLAYDERMAN
COLLECTION

that the artist stay somewhat within the lines of the printed design. Women and children of Liverpool were hired for this work.

Just as the early Dutch and British seamen proudly ordered pictures of their ships to be placed on porcelain by the Cantonese artists, so American sea captains whose ships visited Liverpool could order pottery objects with pictures of their ships and other patriotic devices. Ship designs were used alternately with portraits of American patriots, Masonic devices and other motifs. Occasionally the monogram of the purchaser and the American eagle were placed under the lip of a jug.

As has been pointed out, ceramics with nautical motifs or shapes were most certainly not new to the British potters. Earthenware figures of sailors were popular items for the home market. Creamware jugs with the shipbuilder's arms or with prints of British ships were also made. Two sentimental figural groups enjoyed a long popularity with the British market. These are the well-known "Sailor's Return" and "Sailor's Farewell" that were made by more than one Staffordshire potter.

Most of Great Britain's naval heroes have been commemorated on plates and other ceramic objects, but easily the most frequently extolled hero found on plates, jugs, plaques, etc., is Horatio Nelson. Every anniversary of Nelson's life and death, his ship *Victory* and the Battle of Trafalgar have been the occasion for yet more Nelson-related ceramics.

The War of 1812 and its many sea battles was also cause for printing ceramics with naval motifs. These blue-printed plates, made for the American market, express deep sympathy on the part of the pottery decorators for the American cause. During that war the pottery decorators of England were surprisingly impartial in their tributes to naval heroes of both countries involved. In the potters' zeal to conclude the war and get on with "free trade and sailor's rights," a great many jugs, mugs, punch bowls and plates were decorated with anti-British engravings that would appeal to American customers. A sentiment expressed often on some of the creamware jugs and mugs and on the later blue and white printed tableware is "Success to Trade." The motto often accompanies a portrait of an American ship.

America's naval heroes and the ships they sailed were commemorated on British-made and British-decorated pottery. Subjects were taken from contemporary portraits and engravings that seemed to

British jug with an American hero of the War of 1812, James Lawrence. MATTATUCK MUSEUM

Ship print on a creamware jug and "Success to Trade" with nautical instruments. Made for the American market. MATTATUCK MUSEUM

170

reach the pottery decorators with amazing swiftness. All of the commemoratives of the battles of 1812 are now eagerly sought by marine historians on both sides of the ocean. Those that were printed with subjects sympathetic to the American cause are extremely rare in England. Many were never seen on the British market when they were made, but were shipped abroad immediately upon completion. As was true of the Liverpool printed creamware, British potters used the patriotic devices to ensure a continuation of trade with the important American market.

The early acceptance in the United States of British pottery decorated with patriotic motifs led to a lucrative trade all through the first half of the nineteenth century. British potters realized the necessity for providing acceptable, inexpensive tableware for their customers across the sea. A pottery industry was yet to be established in the United States that could provide any real competition for the imported wares. If national heroes and patriotic scenes were the decoration on the plates, it made little difference to Americans that the plates were produced abroad. Among the blue-printed historical china of the first half of the nineteenth century are many naval and marine scenes. Views of the Hudson River are sought by collectors of ship-decorated objects. Many sea-related scenes were used on the blue and white printed plates made by the Staffordshire potters. The entire history of America's connection with the sea was reproduced, starting with the pottery decorator's version of "The Landing of the Pilgrims at Plymouth Rock" and continuing through to the building of the Erie Canal. Sailing ships and steamships can also be found decorating these early scenes of America.

While the foregoing relates to the importance of British ceramics with marine decoration made for the American market, the Staffordshire potters also made ceramics that would appeal to sailors and their families who lived on British soil. Some of these items were sold as souvenirs at seaport towns, but there was a large enough market at home for these goods. Creamware mugs and bowls were made with the compass rose decoration and "Come Box the Compass" printed on them. A favorite verse that often accompanies the compass design is:

> When this you see
> Remember me,
> Tho' many leagues
> We distant be.

171

"Come Box the Compass" print on a creamware mug, circa 1800. MATTATUCK MUSEUM

Right: This Liverpool printed bowl bears the verse *"When this you see, Remember me, Tho' many leagues, We distant be."* A compass is printed inside, with the phrase, *"Come Box the Compass."* FLAYDERMAN COLLECTION

One eighteenth-century hand-painted, two-handled pot has a colorful picture of a bark. The reverse side carries this sentimental verse:

> Glide on my bark the summer's tide
> Is gently flowing by thy side
> Around thy prow the water's bright
> In circling rounds of broken light.
> Are glitt'ring as if ocean gave
> Her countless gems to deck the wave.

A pink luster mug with platinum luster rim has a ceramic frog attached to the inside bottom. This was a popular gift item in the late eighteenth century. Obviously made to be sold in seaport towns, a verse on the mug reads:

172

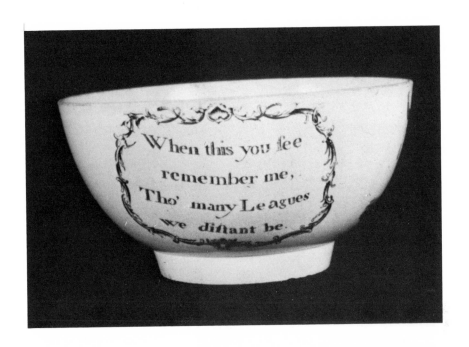

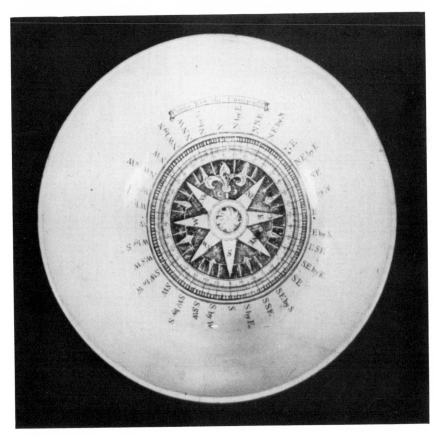

173

Pink luster mug with small ceramic frog on inside bottom and a sentimental nautical verse on the outside.
FLAYDERMAN COLLECTION

The hardy sailor braves the ocean
Fearless of the roaring wind.
Yet his heart with soft emotion
Throbs to leave his love behind.
To dread of foreign foes a stranger
Though youth can, dauntless, roam,
Alarming fears paint every danger
In a rival left at home.

Another popular print for ceramics with "Sailor's Farewell" as a theme shows a sailor's lass returning to shore and the picture is accompanied with this sentimental Victorian verse:

Her light'ning boat unwilling rows to land
Adieu she cry'd and wav'd her lily hand.

174

Another "Sailor's Farewell" luster pitcher has a verse that seems less appropriate for the usual picture of the sailor bidding goodbye to his family. The jug is hand-decorated and has the verse:

> When first I was a foremast man
> I often did pretend
> That if e'er I got promoted
> I would be a seaman's friend
> Then in a little time I was
> Promoted to a mate
> But I then like all the others
> Soon forgot my former state
> And when I became a captain
> I thought myself a King
> And very soon I did forget
> The foremast man I'd been.

Two sides of a Liverpool jug showing printed and hand-painted decorations of an American ship and sailor's girl being rowed ashore. Verse under print reads: "Her light'ning boat unwilling rows to land / Adieu she cry'd and wav'd her lilly hand." Another version of the "Sailor's Farewell."
FLAYDERMAN COLLECTION

This lament about the fickleness of power is accompanied by a design of the mariner's compass flanked by British flags.

The lowly sailor who lost his life at sea was not without his ceramic memorials. A Staffordshire figure of the nineteenth century that was probably all too popular in that period of frequent naval and marine disasters decorated British cottages as a reminder that a member of the family had lost his life at sea. These sailor figurals are inscribed "To the Memory of a Sailor."

It was not only the Chinese and British potters who realized the lucrative market in decorating their wares to appeal to the sailor and the sea-oriented. There were ports besides Liverpool and Canton where ceramics were decorated to order as souvenirs for those who could afford them. Two notable ports where work of this kind was done are Elsinore, Denmark, and Hamburg, Germany. The artists

Mid-nineteenth-century Staffordshire figure, "To the Memory of a Sailor." FLAYDERMAN COLLECTION

Earthenware pitcher with Rockingham glaze and raised design of foul anchor. FLAYDERMAN COLLECTION

Below: Mark found on bowls painted in Elsinore, Denmark. Various decorators signed these bowls, which bore paintings of ships. FLAYDERMAN COLLECTION. *(See color insert)*

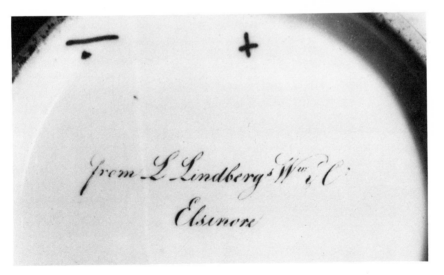

Cup and saucer were hand painted to order by an artist in Hamburg, Germany. Cup bears portrait of a ship, and the saucer the name of the captain. FLAYDERMAN COLLECTION

Mess basin from a British naval vessel, with printed figures of sailors and ships. Basins were stored upside down, which accounts for the mess number being similarly printed. Made in Devon. FLAYDERMAN COLLECTION

who worked at Elsinore and Hamburg undoubtedly solicited business at the waterfront each time a ship came into the harbor. Whatever money was not left at the waterfront drinking establishments by sailors fresh off a ship was probably spent in purchasing these trinkets as souvenirs.

Punch bowls of white porcelain were popular souvenir items of the Elsinore decorators, and their work was of a rather high quality. Each bowl was painted to order with a portrait of a ship or the name and ship of a captain. These Elsinore bowls are handsome and rather difficult to find, although there should be some examples in every nation that used the Danish port in the nineteenth century.

The favorite ceramic shapes for decoration in Germany were small cups and saucers. It was customary for the artist to paint a picture of the ship on which the customer sailed and to paint the name of the captain in the center of the saucer.

There are, of course, many other examples of marine-related antique or old ceramics that have value for the collector. Naval ceramics are one category that can only be touched upon here. Plates and basins of the British Royal Navy are colorfully printed with naval devices, profiles of the reigning king or queen at the time of manufacture, the Crown and mess number. These serviceable printed

Mess plate with portraits of Queen Victoria bordered with nautical vignettes. Devon potter. FLAYDERMAN COLLECTION

Mess plate from the British ship Morgan. *Nautical motifs alternate with floral sprays in border.* FLAYDER-MAN COLLECTION

White ironstone pitcher, as used in ship's mess, with raised design of anchor and American eagle. FLAYDER-MAN COLLECTION

plates were made of heavy earthenware, and many of them were produced in Devon.

Naval ceramics of other seagoing nations are also of importance to the collector. Series of plates made by Wedgwood and other potters in commemoration of naval events and heroes are always sought, as is anything with a marine or naval motif. The field of ceramics collecting in conjunction with the wider area of marine antiques is enormous, and the wares are colorful and of historic importance. Patriotic and personal sentiments abound on ceramics of the sailing-ship era.

15
NAUTICAL MOTIFS
IN THE
DECORATIVE ARTS

The practice of using nautical motifs as decoration for objects to be used on land is as ancient as the history of ships. Greek vases offer glimpses of the ships used in ancient times, and the ship form has been made in silver, glass and porcelain for decorative objects for centuries. In medieval days tableware in the form of small ships, called nefs, was customarily used in families of wealth and nobility to hold salt, which was an expensive commodity worthy of an elaborate vessel. Nefs were made in gold, silver or glass as presentation pieces for the merchants who amassed great fortunes in world trade, and they have become a customary gift for anyone of importance associated with sea life.

The use of the ship as a church decoration is probably one of the oldest examples of ship design for land use. The purpose was certainly more than decorative. The votive paintings, stained glass windows with ship decoration and elaborate ship models that can still be found in some seashore houses of worship were intended as offerings to protect the sailor from harm. Seafarers and their families thought prayers intoned in the presence of a ship representation would have more power.

In any seacoast town in the world, municipal buildings, monuments and churches were all decorated to some extent with the sym-

Nineteenth-century lithograph, "The True Yankee Sailor," had a British counterpart in a popular lithograph "The True British Tar."

THE TRUE YANKEE SAILOR.
A GOOD SHIP & A STIFF BREEZE

Battersea enameled curtain pulls bearing portraits of Commodore Truxton.

American marine hooked rug, made in the late nineteenth century.

Handmade ship weathervane mounted on building in old whaling port of Sag Harbor, Long Island, New York.
LOVELADY POWELL ANTIQUES

Handmade metal and wire ship weathervane from a New England seaport town. SMITHSONIAN INSTITUTION

bols of the trade that was the economic mainstay of the area. In New England whaling towns, weathervanes abound that are patterned after ships, whaling boats, whales, anchors and other marine devices. Trade signs in the figure of a sailor announced a chandler's shop or the local maker of navigational instruments. A sign in the shape of a fish told the sailor that he could purchase bait and tackle in an establishment on the waterfront. An elaborate ship model weathervane often announced the shipyard location on the waterfront.

The sailor and the fisherman have been subjects for the sculptor throughout history. The small bronzes of the late Victorian era with marine subjects attest to the custom of nineteenth-century artists to romanticize life on or near the sea.

The clockmaker has used sea and ship designs in painted form, such as the early clocks with reverse-glass paintings, or as sculptural devices to embellish a case. Although the eighteenth-century clocks with reverse-glass paintings of ships are difficult to find today, later turn-of-the-century clocks decorated with three-dimensional nautical devices such as those illustrated in this book are now considered

Late nineteenth-century copper fish trade sign, used to advertise New England bait and tackle shop. SHELBURNE MUSEUM

Two anchors form the decoration for window grill or transom of waterfront building. HEART AND STAR ANTIQUES

Small bronze statue of a fisherman carrying an anchor. FLAYDERMAN COLLECTION,

186

Small bronze of two fishermen in oilskins hauling line. American, early twentieth century. FLAYDERMAN COLLECTION

Nautical designs form brass and bronze clock on marble base. Marked R. Kirkpatrick, New York. FLAYDERMAN COLLECTION

Large turn-of-the-century brass clock with nautical devices, including lifeboat, anchors, blocks and ropes.
FLAYDERMAN COLLECTION

worthwhile investments. One is a fascinating combination of a ship's light, blocks and ropes, ship's wheels, capstans and anchors—all in miniature. This clock was made to appeal to the ship buff and might have been intended to decorate a ship or yacht club. It is of American make and is marked *R. Kirkpatrick, New York*. Anchors, ship's wheels, ropes and blocks and other nautical devices have been incorporated into every form of the decorative arts.

Marine motifs have decorated various types of domestic glassware

*Brass candlesticks with an-
chor design.* FLAYDERMAN
COLLECTION

*Goblet, elaborately etched, and com-
memorative of Admiral Lord Nelson.*
FLAYDERMAN COLLECTION

189

Left: American pressed glass pitcher, a naval commemorative for Admiral Dewey, hero of the Spanish-American War. Right: Decanter with ship and etched inscription "Homeward Bound." BOTH PHOTOS: FLAYDERMAN COLLECTION

for many years. Presentation goblets to celebrate a ship's launching have been made throughout the history of shipbuilding, and glass presentation commemoratives honoring naval heroes can also be found. Many of these are superb examples of the glass-blower's and engraver's art. Decanters made for use on naval vessels of various nations are usually decorated with maritime symbols and national insignia and are often of superb quality.

Stamps and coins of every seafaring nation in the world have been designed with ships or other nautical devices that commemorate the history of each country's vessels and the men who sailed in them. Of particular interest to specialist stamp collectors are the ship cancellations of the nineteenth century. In the days before government-regulated postal carriers, packet boats carried mail along with other cargo. Letters were often entrusted to sea captains for delivery to their ports of call. Knowledgeable philatelists and postal historians are aware of the importance of the early ship cancellations on letters that were "mailed" long before postage stamps came into common use. Frequently these letters gave their recipient detailed instructions on how to send a return letter by ship.

Tapestries, paintings and prints all record the history of the sailing ship, but these are a complicated study in themselves. Nautical devices as well as marine life have decorated furniture from early times. All sea-related designs have appeared periodically throughout the history of the decorative arts. It is said that Lady Hamilton endeared

Left: United States Navy decanter. Note eagle sitting on anchor. FLAYDERMAN COLLECTION *Right: Shells were used for making elaborate flowers and flower arrangements during the Victorian period. It is probable that seafarers brought colorful shells back from voyages for this purpose.* SUFFOLK COUNTY WHALING MUSEUM

herself to Nelson early in their association by dressing from head to toe in fabric designed with nautical motifs.

The influence of a particular naval hero, or an especially strong association of a member of royalty with his country's navy, will make nautical devices more popular in fashion. The custom of dressing children in sailor suits reached an all-time high during the Edwardian era. Every well-dressed boy at the turn of the century wore a sailor suit. The sailor's hat and nautical fashion reappear periodically in the history of women's dress.

The sea has provided inspiration for craftsmen and artists for centuries. The ships, the men who sailed in them and the symbolic designs that represent sea life have figured in religious and secular art throughout civilization. Those objects that represent the days of sail and the early development of the steam-powered vessels deserve an important place in the story of mankind. All fit together to tell us about the great adventures of sailing and sea travel.

Tin biscuit box with print of the Constitution, *probably made between 1909 and 1920 when the ship was being restored.* AUTHOR'S COLLECTION

16
STEAMSHIP RELICS

Because the sailing ship survived through most of the nineteenth century, it is difficult to believe that the idea of the steamship was far enough advanced in Lord Nelson's lifetime for him to have written to the Admiralty that a steam-driven boat launched in France by Robert Fulton would bear watching. The sailing ship most certainly did not become obsolete when Fulton launched his first commercially successful steamboat, the *Clermont* (possibly called the *North River*) on the Hudson River in 1807.

Fulton's steamboat was followed by Henry Ball's *Comet* in 1812. Seven years later came the first steamship to cross the Atlantic, the American-built *Savannah*, which had auxiliary steam power, used for only about 85 hours during her passage of 27½ days from Savannah, Georgia to Liverpool. Fuel consumption was still so high that a ship could not carry enough to last over a long journey unless sails were used when the wind was right.

The first two ships to cross the Atlantic solely under steam power were the 703-ton *Sirius* and the 1,320-ton *Great Western*, both of which reached New York within a few hours of each other in April 1838. The *Great Western* had steamed continuously for 15 days 5 hours at an average speed of 8.8 knots. However, all ships continued to carry auxiliary sails until the *Great Britain* was launched in 1834. It was the invention of the screw propeller, as adopted by the *Great Britain*, that was to make ocean steam travel practicable throughout the latter half of the nineteenth century. With the subsequent introduction of the turbine engine and its later refinements, the sailing ship for ocean travel was doomed.

Tobacco jar in shape of a capstan, commemorative of Admiral Dewey and his flagship, Olympia. FLAY-DERMAN COLLECTION

American pressed glass ships were made to "Remember the Maine." FLAY-DERMAN COLLECTION

Half-hull model of an American sidewheeler set against a painted panoramic background. FLAYDERMAN COLLECTION

Power-driven vessels have their own literature and history, and the great ships that have met with disaster attest to the fact that there are still some risks involved in sea travel. We tend to romanticize the history of the sailing ship, but as more great ocean liners are retired than are being built, it becomes obvious that transoceanic luxury ship travel will someday be a thing of the past. There has been a tendency in recent years to preserve relics of the early steamship days along with those of the sailing ships.

The great luxurious floating hotels of this century are slowly but surely being replaced by the airplane and already relics from the *Queen Mary* and her sister ship, the *Queen Elizabeth*, are being collected. It should be obvious to any maritime historian that any identifiable souvenir from the latter ship, which caught fire in Hong Kong in 1971 while being outfitted as a floating college, will someday be of value. Fortunately, the *Queen Mary* has been preserved intact and is now a maritime museum in California. Both of these great ships served long lifetimes as luxury liners and as troop carriers in

Wheelboard from sidewheeler, which helped to keep decks and passengers from being splashed. Carved with lighthouse design. FLAYDERMAN COLLECTION

World War II, and they represent a peak in the history of twentieth-century ocean travel.

If interest came too late to save even one American clipper ship, there have been some efforts made to preserve examples of the American sidewheeler steamboats. The ship *Ticonderoga*, built in 1906 for travel on Lake Champlain, was in service until 1950, when it was permanently docked through the efforts of a citizens' committee, and turned into a floating museum. After a few years it proved too expensive to keep the ship afloat, so the *Ticonderoga* was moved to the grounds of the Shelburne Museum in Vermont, where it is now on display.

Other examples of the steamboat are being preserved in the United States. A few Mississippi paddlewheelers still survive, and one or two are presently in operation as excursion boats. Ships of the Great Lakes area have been turned into tourist attractions, and a few historic American battleships have become museums. The steamboat *Fall River Line* is housed indoors at Fall River, Massachusetts. In it are displayed models and other memorabilia of the days of marine steam power.

Collectors who are interested in relics of the steamship days look for trade cards and posters that advertise the early steamship lines. The colorful trade cards of this era, more easily accessible than the clipper ship cards, evolved in the late nineteenth century into the picture postcards that were popular at the time. A collection of these cards, given away as advertisements by the shipping lines, forms a colorful record of inland and transoceanic steamship travel.

One interesting variety of the shipline picture postcard is the menu card. These were ships' menus with the top half a picture postcard that could be torn off and mailed aboard ship. Other nautical postcards for the collector that are now in great demand are the jacquard-woven silk ship portraits made in England and France at the beginning of this century.

Perhaps the most desirable of all relics of the earlier steamship days are name boards and paddlewheel covers. Frequently the latter were carved or painted in a decorative manner. Covers for the side-wheelers were a necessity since they kept the water from splashing onto the deck.

Ceramics, glassware and other decorative objects associated with the day-line boats or the ocean liners from the earlier part of this

Advertising calendar tiles made by Wedgwood depict the Cunard Line Dock and the Boston Customs House. JO-ANNE BLUM, INC.

Small advertising card of Boston's State Steam Ship Company, showing dock scene. FLAYDERMAN COLLECTION

Advertising card for National Line Steamships. FLAYDERMAN COLLECTION

Right: Fred W. Leighton, British ship artist, designed postcards for collectors, which were printed by Raphael Tuck & Co. POSTCARD MUSEUM

Advertising card for Guion Line, United States Mail Steamers. FLAYDERMAN COLLECTION

Postcards cut from the tops of ships' menus helped to advertise the shipping company. POSTCARD MUSEUM

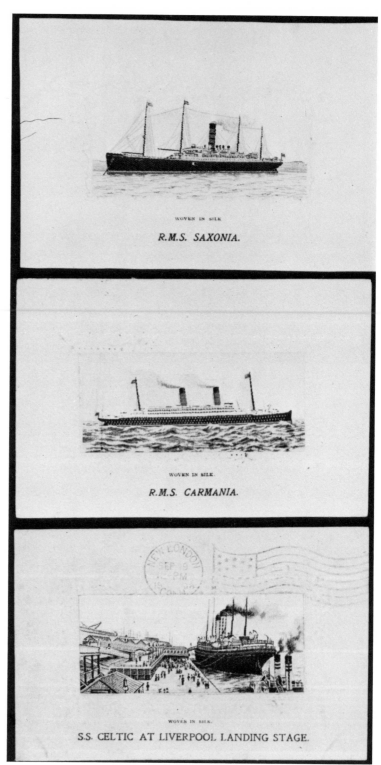

Postcards of ship portraits woven on jacquard looms were popular at the beginning of the present century. POST-CARD MUSEUM

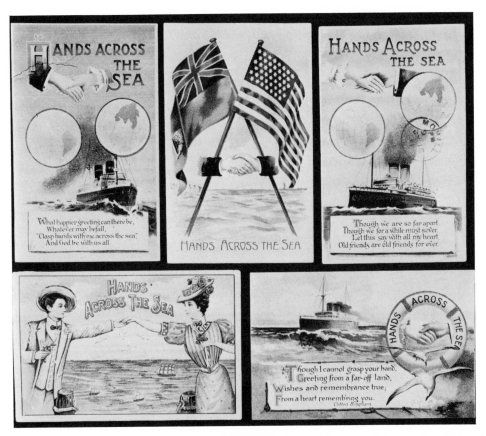

Pre-World War I postcards stressed friendship between England and the United States, and were popular with collectors of that period. POSTCARD MUSEUM

century are also available for the collector of ship memorabilia. Obviously, any relics connected with famous ships that met disastrous ends are important historical documentary material. Advertising material and anything else that relates to the ill-fated maiden voyage of the *Titanic* is, of course, of the greatest interest to marine historians.

While the sidewheelers, sternwheelers and luxury ocean liners do not fire the imagination of the collector in the same way that the whaling ships, clippers and other early sailing vessels do, they are all important in world maritime history. It is fortunate that many collectors and museums now have the foresight to preserve as much of this history as possible.

17

THE GOLDEN AGE
OF YACHTING

For lovers of the sea there are few more beautiful sights in the world than a sailing regatta. The luxury of sailing for sport and recreation is one that until recently has been confined to a very small segment of the world's population. Yacht races of old were usually one boat and crew pitted against another, each also racing against time and the elements. It is thought that the first such race in England was probably the match between the yacht *Katherine*, owned by Charles II, and the yacht *Anne*, owned by the Duke of York. This race took place on 1 October, 1662.

The first recorded sailing regatta, from Westminster Bridge to Putney Bridge, was sponsored by the Duke of Cumberland in 1775. The Cumberland Cup race led to the formation of the Cumberland Society, which later became the Royal Thames Yacht Club. Yacht racing had been known in Holland, however, since the early seventeenth century. The first formally organized yachting club was founded in Ireland in 1720. The oldest organization in the United States devoted to the sport of yachting and yacht racing is the New York Yacht Club, founded in 1844.

During the nineteenth and early twentieth centuries yachting became a popular sport among the wealthy, but from the spectator's point of view it was national in nature. By present standards, these early yachts were very large. They were often over one hundred feet long, carried professional crews and were, of course, used for pleasure cruising as well as in competition.

202

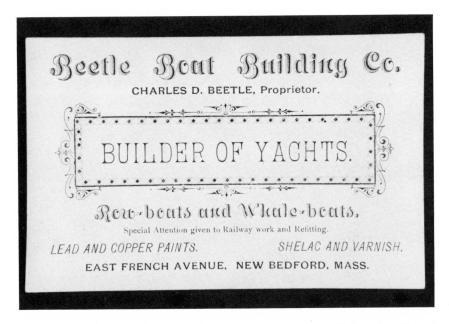

The first international yachting event, sponsored by the Royal Yacht Squadron of England, took place in 1851. The race was open to competitors from all nations. Sixteen yachts took part in the event. This famous race, around the Isle of Wight, was won by the *America* and the trophy, presented by the Royal Yacht Squadron and originally called the Hundred Guinea Cup, became known there-

Above: Business card of the New Bedford "Beetle Boat Building Co." announcing yachts as their major product. FLAYDERMAN COLLECTION

Right: Brass button from New York Yacht Club blazer, late nineteenth century.

Silver cup awarded for a yacht race won by the sloop Gracie *on June 20, 1872. Note anchor and rope decoration.* FLAYDERMAN COLLECTION

after as "The *America's* Cup." It was presented to the New York Yacht Club as an international challenge cup, to be raced for every year. The cup, a bulbous, bottomless, ewer-shaped silver trophy, has never left America since its arrival, for though there have been a number of challenges, none has yet been successful.

Yacht racing as a sport has always been avidly followed, if not actively participated in, by rich and poor alike. In many areas of the world where the great races are still held, the magnificent sight of billowing sails can still be observed on the day of an important race. Competition for the America's Cup, the Seawanhaka Cup, the Canada's Cup and the Scandinavian Gold Cup are events of great importance to the sporting sailor. From the Tall Ships' Race in North European waters, to the Paris Six Hour Speedboat race on the Seine, there is an excitement that is unsurpassed in any other form of sport competition. However, for the sailing buff there is no event more appealing than a race of sailing craft of any class.

Today there are thousands of yacht clubs all over the world. The "yachts" range from small sloops and half-decked motor cruisers to diesel-powered oceangoing vessels and large schooners. The hobby is popular on any body of water, from lakes and rivers to bays and oceans. The great luxury sailing yachts of the nineteenth century and the beginning of this century have all but disappeared, and yachting historians search for objects representing those symbols of enormous wealth.

Silver cup awarded for match race between the Gracie *and the* Mita *over a 20-mile course from Sandy Hook and back on July 23, 1872.* FLAYDERMAN COLLECTION

In the history of yachting there are, of course, outstanding vessels that were legendary in their time for the associations with successful racing records or with the famous men who owned them. Collectors seek ship's wheels, marine instruments and other furnishings that were often ornamental as well as practical, plus models of the famous craft. Trophies of races won in the nineteenth and early twentieth centuries are also sought. These are of interest because they were specially designed decorative silver pieces made in the many ornate styles of the nineteenth century and often adorned with nautical motifs.

All souvenirs of famous yachting events of the nineteenth century should be preserved as part of the history of this exclusive sport. These mementos of the affluence and gentlemanly competition of this rather exclusive branch of maritime history are somewhat more difficult to find than many other examples of marine antiques from the same period but the specialty provides a challenge welcomed by the really keen collector.

18

THE CARE
AND REPAIR OF
MARINE ANTIQUES

Museums and collectors face similar problems concerning the restoration and preservation of marine antiques. For the few maritime museums in ownership of an early sailing vessel, the obligations in continuous restoration and upkeep are very great and the expense enormous. When these ships are kept afloat there is constant need for replacement of wood, repainting and refurbishing. Whether the ship is used as a floating museum or permanently moored in a dock, the elements continue to take their toll as though the ship were still in active service. Because of this, it is little wonder that so few of the early sailing ships have been preserved. As noted earlier, in the case of some of the restorations of this type, money has been raised by public subscription or by selling souvenir fragments from pieces removed in restoring the ship.

The most recent attempt at this important type of ship restoration has been going on for a period of ten years on the United States frigate *Constellation*. She is the only survivor of fifteen hundred ships that comprised the Union Navy, and she participated in the Civil War. During the early years of World War II the *Constellation* served as the flagship of the North Atlantic Fleet, but by 1954 all that was left of her was a rotting hulk, Rear Admiral Donald F. Stewart, working with members of the U.S. Congress, managed to have a bill passed to purchase and restore the ship as close as possible to the state she was in when built in 1797. Besides government funds procured for this extensive restoration, medals were struck in silver and bronze and sold to augment existing funds.

This is an example of the ultimate in restoration of a marine antique. However, for the collector, the more immediate problems in the area of care and repair of nautical collectibles pertain to the categories of ship figureheads and other carvings, scrimshaw and ship models. Restoration of these three categories of collectors' items requires special information and handling.

The wood of ships has been exposed to salt, sun and water to a degree not usual with wood from land architecture, and the conservation of painted and carved wooden ship decoration presents certain rather serious problems. In making a decision as to whether a figurehead or other ship carving should be restored as closely as possible to its original state or left in the weathered condition in which it is usually found, the collector, and especially the museum curator, should consider each possibility carefully.

In the case of a museum acquisition, a policy should be established that would cover all carved ship objects in the collection. Obviously, there is always a great deal of soul-searching involved concerning the amount of restoration an object such as a ship's figurehead should be given. In many collections the figureheads are displayed in their "found" condition. That is, the wood is treated to prevent further deterioration, but no attempt is made to present the figureheads as they looked when they were new. This philosophy seems to be most prevalent in American museums. The superb collection at Mystic Seaport in Connecticut is an example of the great effort expended to preserve, but not change, the ship carvings.

Wood retains moisture in a manner similar to a sponge. Removing a ship's carving from its normal damp environment and exposing it to interior heat can cause rapid drying and deterioration. Therefore, careful handling is required before a ship's carving can be safely placed in an interior environment. Many carved wooden figures have been damaged by dry rot. These affected pieces of wood must be cut out and matching pieces made and artificially weathered as replacements. This work should be attempted only by experts, for it often requires major surgery not only in the rotted wood but in the surrounding areas as well. The wood grain and type must be perfectly matched, and the carving of these replacement pieces requires a talent no less developed than that of the original figurehead carver.

There are methods for treating wood chemically to prevent further rot and to preserve any remaining vestiges of the original paint and gilding. Some of these methods are irreversible if applied in the wrong manner or amount, and most are dangerous for an amateur to use. While the usual wood preventatives against dry rot and insects—such as creosote—are helpful when there is no damage, they are of little use in repairing already existing damage. A waterlogged figurehead must be dried out very slowly and carefully, keeping the object damp to prevent it from drying too fast and ultimately cracking or rotting. Other methods, such as freeze-drying, require special equipment or the use of dangerous chemicals.

Any old ship figurehead is worth preserving. Each is unique and an example of original folk carving, and all are a part of the world's maritime history. Private collectors and museum personnel have an obligation to see that all restoration is done with as much care as possible. It would be wise for the private collector who owns a figurehead that is in need of restoration to consult the nearest maritime museum for the name of a craftsman knowledgeable in this very specialized field of wood preservation.

While most figurehead collections in American museums are displayed as weathered artifacts, figureheads in other parts of the world have been painstakingly restored to their original new state. This type of restoration is very costly and requires careful research and a knowledge of paint chemistry. In addition, someone must be found who can paint the figurehead in a manner typical of the period in which it was originally made.

A figurehead or other ship carving that has been badly repainted diminishes considerably in value and certainly loses much of its attractiveness. One example of superb restoration can be found in the collection at the outdoor museum at Tresco in the Isles of Scilly. Open sheds protect the collection to some extent from the elements, but the restoration they have been given should lengthen the lives of the carvings considerably. The philosophy at Tresco has been to restore the figureheads and other ships' carvings to look as nearly original as when they were new. Replacement of rotted wood parts was only the beginning for this type of ambitious project. Paint samples were carefully studied and analyzed, and new paint was made to match the original as closely as possible. Skin tones in particular were carefully analyzed, and the Tresco figureheads now appear much as they did when first made. A single figurehead has been left unrestored for comparison. Since figureheads were repainted as often as the ships that carried them, restorers must often do careful and painstaking research to discover the original colors and type of paint used. Restoration under these conditions requires a skilled workman and artist.

Because of the expense involved in restoring or preserving carved wood from ships, it is important that the collector take these costs into consideration before he purchases a ship's carving that has previously received no restorative attention. Obviously, due to the rarity on the market of figureheads and early ship's carvings, any effort spent on preserving the relatively few that survive today is well worthwhile.

The tooth of the whale is a sturdy and stable material, and part of the charm of old scrimshaw is that it has yellowed and developed a patina that is impossible to duplicate in new work. This yellowed surface is one way of telling old scrimshaw from the new, and no effort should be made to bleach or wash a scrimshawed tooth. Scrimshawed objects from baleen or panbone should also be left as is. All scrimshaw should be kept away from direct sunlight and most certainly as far from radiators as possible.

Dirt can be removed from scrimshawed objects with a dry brush. Stubborn dirt can be further treated by dipping a cotton swab into a solution of detergent and water, but the object must be dried immediately. In no case should water be allowed to remain on the surface, for moisture is damaging to any ivory. In addition, many of the coloring agents used by sailors in scrimshaw work were not waterproof. It would be distressing to wash away the brown shades that were achieved by rubbing tobacco juice into a scratched design. Generally, one should leave all ivory objects alone and simply attempt to prevent any further deterioration from exposure to excessive heat or light.

Whalebone objects other than the scrimshawed teeth may need minor repair. The one scrimshawed object most often in need of repair is the tableswift. The thin ribs, if broken, will probably stay together with an application of white glue. Be certain that all excess glue is wiped off before it dries. Reinforcement with wire, tape or string will hold the two pieces together until the glue has set. If the hinges have worn or broken, match the wire or string used to hold the ribs to the swift as closely as possible to the original material (note that silver wire was sometimes used for this purpose).

The bone from which prisoners of war made ship models was taken from animals other than the whale. However, the same rules for care and repair should be followed. Since most of these valuable models have been protected in glass cases, few have deteriorated to any extent. In no instance should they be exposed to sunlight, heat or water.

Ship models require the most attention in the area of restoration. Depending upon the degree of deterioration and neglect to which a model has been exposed, proper repair of sails, masts and rigging may consume many hours of effort and patience. When these parts of a model are in a particularly jumbled state, it would be advisable to find a diagram, painting or engraving of the type of ship that most closely resembles your model. If it is of a well-known ship still in existence—such as the *Cutty Sark*, the *Victory*, the *Constitution* or the *Charles W. Morgan*, all of which have been preserved—it is possible

Rerigging a bone and wood model such as this one of the C. W. Morgan *is a tricky job calling for expert knowledge and unlimited patience.*

211

to obtain a photograph that will show exactly the proper arrangement of masts, sails and rigging. Carefully study the rigging of the particular ship or a diagram that most resembles your model to be certain what replacements will be required.

All rigging must be taut to create the desired effect. Note that all British ships before 1870 had rope rigging; ships built after that date had wire rigging. Most ship model builders use the following types of rigging: linen cord for halyards and sheets; thread fishline for shrouds, stays and topping lifts; sewing thread for downhauls and light lines.

Tools and materials needed to repair rigging are a pair of tweezers, scissors, needles and thread and a bottle of white glue. You can add stiffness to thread rigging by drawing the thread through a piece of beeswax and passing it quickly over a flame.

Replacing sails on a ship model also requires an understanding of the type of ship the model represents and an idea of when that type of ship was built. Since we are speaking here of replacing only one or two sails that have become rotted or torn, an effort will have to be made to match the material used on the model for sails. It will be necessary to attempt to age the new cloth. Plain white cotton cloth or an opaque linen were the materials generally used for sailmaking on models. American ship sails were made from white canvas, while European sails were usually made from unbleached linen. However, most model-makers "aged" their sails, or the sails on an old model may have yellowed. The repairer can achieve a similar effect by dipping the sail replacement into a pan of strong coffee or tea, or by spraying the finished sail with a tinted lacquer or stain.

With all ship model repairs, an effort should be made to restore the model as closely as possible to its original condition. A badly torn sail can be replaced by using the old fragments as a pattern for a new one. Try to duplicate the degree of completeness and exactness of detail. If hems, buntlines and clew lines were used, follow the original model-maker's methods and amount of detail. Be certain that all sail replacements are in scale with the ship and the rest of the sails.

Some ingenuity will be required to replace any missing parts on a ship model. Study the remaining pieces to identify the methods used by the original model-maker in adapting or making miniature parts for a ship. Brass battery nuts were often used as capstans, and davits were sometimes made from fishhooks. Throughout the history of ship model-making, ingenious ways have been found to adapt ordinary household articles as parts of a ship.

There are many books and articles relating to ship model building. Before any attempt is made to do a major overhaul job on an old and valuable model, these should be read carefully. The greatest help is to find a diagram of the ship or type of ship your model represents and to work from that. If the repairs necessary to make your model shipshape require many hours of patience, remember that the more elaborate ship models sometimes took their makers many thousands of hours of patient work. Any effort spent in restoring these works of art is certainly worth the time, study and patience.

Well-constructed, accurate handmade ship models are becoming more valuable every day, and careful restoration adds to the value of a ship model. There are still dedicated model-makers capable of doing complicated repairs if you are reluctant to tackle the job yourself. Old and accurate ship models in good repair are in constant demand by collectors. In many cases a model may be the only record we have that a particular ship existed at all. For this reason any model made contemporaneously with the ship it represents is of importance to historians as well as collectors and certainly should be kept in good condition.

19

FAKES, REPRODUCTIONS AND RECENTLY MADE COLLECTIBLES

A collector of relics of the old sailing days may argue that little of importance can be found outside of museums today. Furthermore, the experienced collector knows he is competing for any important objects that do come on the market with museums as well as collectors of other specialties that transcend the marine aspect of the objects. For instance, any autograph collector would be interested in acquiring whaling-ship papers or letters of marque signed by important public figures in history.

The coin and medal collector is aware that certain of the lifesaving awards and national medals were designed by important sculptors. And one does not have to be a lover of marine antiques to know that anything connected with the history of Western trade with China is of value for its artistic as well as its historic aspects. The collector of antique ceramics or glass will compete with the collector specializing only in marine antiques for a Liverpool pitcher or a launching goblet. There are so many enthusiasts of early advertising items that the collector of marine antiques has a lot of competition in purchasing ship posters or clipper-ship sailing cards. All folk art is in great demand in the various countries to which it is indigenous, and it is becoming increasingly difficult to find rare documented examples of the sailor's art.

In addition to these problems, the great demand for marine antiques has led to the manufacture of many fakes and reproductions. Marine objects have always been held in high esteem by collectors, and the more desirable items that have historically brought the highest prices have been reproduced for many years. Ships' carvings, among the most decorative of all maritime antiques, have been made by obliging woodcarvers in recent years and placed on the market as old. Carved wood is difficult to date, especially when it is painted, and it would be wise for the collector to keep this in mind. He should take every opportunity to study museum collections, and make any purchase of ship carvings from a reputable dealer.

Many of the plainer eighteenth-century charts were painted by hand at a later date to appeal to collectors. There is often no way to distinguish charts that have original handpainting from those that were doctored at a later date. But there are methods of detecting a completely new chart reproduced from old plates.

All paper ephemera can be duplicated rather easily. Clipper-ship sailing cards are currently being reprinted, but as far as can be ascertained, these are only being used as current picture postcards, which should create no problem for the knowledgeable collector. However, it should be noted that there is strong demand among American collectors for these colorful lithographs, and the high prices the originals are currently commanding might encourage some forgeries.

Ship models have been made for centuries and are still being built today by hobbyists. Many of these are as carefully planned, built and rigged as those that are two hundred years old or more. A good ship model still requires many hours of painstaking work. However, it is important for the collector considering purchasing a model to know when it was built in order to have some idea of its value. Obviously, a model constructed contemporaneously with the ship it represents is of more value than one made yesterday, no matter how much they might resemble each other. This is of little importance to someone purchasing a model simply for its decorative appeal, but vital to the serious collector of maritime antiques.

To distinguish old models from new ones, it is necessary to know something of the construction methods used by early model builders and of the fabric used for sails and rigging. If in doubt about a ship model that has no provenance, have it checked by an expert before making a major investment.

While it is often difficult to authenticate many handcrafted items as to age, etched whales' teeth that have some age will show a dark patina or yellowing. There have been many new pieces of scrimshaw placed on the market recently in America, but these are whiter than the old examples and the etching is generally rather simple and poorly executed. Other examples of sailors' crafts seem not to have been reproduced in any amount. The knowledge needed to make the fancy ropework handles of sailors' chests has been lost to us, and it is unlikely that this aspect of marine art will appear as fakes or forgeries. Moreover, the beckets show a great amount of age from constant handling, and one can assume that any found today are old and authentic.

There are many recently made ceramic ship commemoratives, all of which are worth collecting. Notable ceramics of this type were made during the 1970 celebration of the 350th anniversary of the landing of the Pilgrims at Plymouth, Massachusetts. The anniversary was commemorated in the old tradition by British potters such as

Mayflower *cup made by* Wedgwood *in 1970 to commemorate the 350th anniversary of the ship's voyage to America.* COURTESY JOSIAH WEDGWOOD AND SONS, LTD.

*"Old Ironsides," a Wedg-
wood commemorative
plate.* AUTHOR'S COLLECTION

Wedgwood, and several exceptional contemporary designs were
made for that occasion. These are all produced in limited numbers.
Although not in the "antique" category, they can become a part of
any maritime collection of ceramics.

During this century other ceramics with maritime motifs were
made that might be considered by the collector of nautical ceramics.
Many of these were designed by outstanding artists. The plates and
other objects will someday be of importance similar to that of the
Liverpool pitchers and other earlier collectibles. Among these are a
series of plates called "Historical Canadian Vessels" and another
called "American Sailing Ships."

Among a series of plates designed for Wedgwood by the woodcut
artist Clare Leighton, is one that commemorates the New England
whaling industry. Although contemporary in design, it is still in the
old tradition of marine ceramics made by the British potters for the
American market. It must be emphasized that these twentieth-century ceramics are in no way fakes or reproductions, but historic
commemoratives of importance to the collector of maritime objects.

217

Blue and white jasperware by Wedgwood commemorating the anniversary of the founding of Bermuda. JOHN S. COE COLLECTION

Columbia, *a plate from the "American Sailing Ship Series" made by Wedgwood in contemporary style but in the old tradition of British potters.* AUTHOR'S COLLECTION

"Whaling," print for a plate design produced by artist Clare Leighton for a Wedgwood series called "New England Industries." CLARE LEIGHTON

The inexperienced beginning collector of nautical antiques should make every effort to study the field and learn the history of ships and sailing. He should take every opportunity to visit the great museum collections available throughout the world, and should not make any major investments until he is thoroughly acquainted with the many aspects of the hobby. It might be wise to specialize in only one type of item since the field is vast. It will take a lot of knowledge and experience before it becomes easy to recognize good or inferior examples and to know the poor investments from the wise. The dealers who specialize in marine antiques are among the most knowledge-

219

able of all sea historians, and the serious collector would benefit from confining his purchases only to reputable dealers.

Whether one's interest in marine history focuses on world trade, naval warfare, ship architecture, marine archeology, navigational instruments, the development of the fishing industries throughout the world, maritime exploration or simply the decorative aspects of the objects that represent all of these fields, there is a wealth of material still available in every seafaring nation of the world. For those who love the sea there can be no more satisfying hobby than to collect and preserve for future generations those objects that represent the romance, lore and myths of man's ability to conquer the world's oceans.

MARITIME MUSEUMS
OF THE WORLD

The following is a list of maritime museums. In addition to these museums, all of which have permanent marine exhibits, there are many smaller collections in general museums and historical societies.

ARGENTINA
Tigre, Provincia de Buenos Aires
    Museo Naval de la Nación

AUSTRALIA
Melbourne
    Institute of Applied Science of
    Victoria

BELGIUM
Antwerp
    National Scheepvaartmuseum

CANADA
St John, New Brunswick
    The New Brunswick Museum
Vancouver
    Vancouver Maritime Museum

DENMARK
Copenhagen
    Orlogmuseet

Helsingør
    Danish Maritime Museum

GREAT BRITAIN
England
London
    Science Museum, South
        Kensington
    National Maritime Museum,
        Greenwich
    Imperial War Museum
Bristol
    Maritime Museum
Devonshire
    Exeter Maritime Museum
    Brixham Maritime Museum
    Plymouth Dockyard and Town
Durham
    Hartlepool Maritime Museum
    Sunderland Maritime Museum
Hampshire
    Portsmouth: Royal Naval

Museum, comprising two
collections, 'Victory' and
'Nelson', the latter donated
by Mrs. J. G. McCarthy,
CBE; Royal Marines Museum;
Submarine Museum (*HMS
Dolphin*)
Beaulieu: Bucklers Hard
Maritime Museum
Bournemouth: Rothesay
Museum
Southampton: Maritime
Museum
Isle of Man
Castletown: Nautical Museum
Douglas: The Manx Museum
Isles of Scilly
Tresco: Valhalla Museum
St Mary's: Isles of Scilly
Museum
Lancashire
City of Liverpool Museum
Norfolk
Great Yarmouth: Maritime
Museum for East Anglia
Northumberland
Newcastle-upon-Tyne Museum
Yorkshire
Whitby Maritime Museum
Hull Maritime Museum
Kingston-upon-Hull Maritime
Museum: collections of Hull
whaling industry (including
scrimshaw) , ship models,
figureheads, nautical
instruments, etc.
Wales
Monmouthshire
Monmouth: Nelson Museum
Scotland
Angus
Broughty Castle: (Dundee
whaling)

Fife
Anstruther (Scottish Fisheries
Museum)
Lanarkshire
Glasgow Art Gallery and
Museum
Midlothian
Edinburgh: Royal Scottish
Museum

FINLAND
Mariehamn
Ålands Sjöfartsmuseum

FRANCE
Marseilles
Musée Maritime
Paris
Musée de la Marine
Saint-Malo
Musée de Saint-Malo

GERMANY
Brake/Unterweser
Schiffahrts-Museum
Hamburg
Altonaer Museum
Munich
Deutsches Museum

HOLLAND
Amsterdam
Nederlansch Historisch
Scheepvart Museum
Rijksmuseum
Rotterdam
Maritiem Museum "Prins
Hendrik''

ICELAND
Reykjavik
National Museum of Iceland

ISRAEL
Haifa
  Maritime Museum

ITALY
Genoa-Pegli
  Musèo Navale
Trieste
  Musè del Mare
Venice
  Musèo Storico Navale

JAPAN
Tokyo
  Transportation Museum

NORWAY
Oslo
  Kon-Tiki Museum
Sandefjord
  Sandefjord Sjøfartsmuseum
  Kommander Chr.
    Christensen's
    Hvalfangstmuseum

PORTUGAL
Lisbon
  Museo de Marinha

SPAIN
Barcelona
  Museo Maritimo
Madrid
  Museo Naval

SWEDEN
Göteborg
  Sjöfartsmuseet
Karlskrona
  Marinmuseum
Stockholm
  Statens Sjöhistoriska

SWITZERLAND
Lucerne
  Swiss Transport Museum

U.S.S.R.
Leningrad
  Naval Museum

UNITED STATES
California
San Francisco
  San Francisco Maritime
    Museum
  San Francisco Maritime State
    Historic Park
Connecticut
Mystic
  Mystic Seaport
District of Columbia
  Smithsonian Institution
  Truxton-Decatur Naval
    Museum
Georgia
Savannah
  Ships of the Sea Museum
Iowa
Keokuk
  Keokuk River Museum
Maine
Bath
  Bath Maritime Museum
Searsport
  Penobscot Marine Museum
Maryland
Annapolis
  United States Naval Academy
    Museum
St Michaels
  Chesapeake Bay Maritime
    Museum
Massachusetts
Boston
  Museum of Science

Cambridge
  Francis Russell Hart Nautical
    Museum
Edgartown
  Thomas Cook House and
    Museum
Fall River
  Marine Museum of Fall River
Milton
  Museum of the American
    China Trade
Nantucket
  Whaling Museum
New Bedford
  Whaling Museum
Salem
  Peabody Museum of Salem
Michigan
Dearborn
  Henry Ford Museum and
    Greenfield Village
Detroit
  Dossin Great Lakes Museum
Mackinaw City
  Mackinac Maritime Park
New York
Clayton
  Thousand Islands Museum
  Thousand Islands Shipyard
    Museum
Cold Spring Harbor
  Whaling Museum
New York City
  South Street Seaport Museum
Sag Harbor
  Suffolk County Whaling
    Museum
Whitehall
  Skenesborough Museum

North Carolina
Carolina Beach
  Blockade Runner Museum
Ohio
Marietta
  Campus Martius Museum
Oregon
Astoria
  Columbia River Maritime
    Museum
Pennsylvania
Philadelphia
  Philadelphia Maritime Museum
Texas
Fredericksburg
  Admiral Nimitz Center
Vermont
Shelburne
  Shelburne Museum
Virginia
Newport News
  Mariners Museum
Portsmouth
  Portsmouth Naval Shipyard
    Museum
Washington
Seattle
  Northwest Seaport
Wisconsin
Manitowoc
  Manitowoc Maritime Museum

YUGOSLAVIA
Dubrovnik
  Maritime Museum of the
    Yugoslav Academy of the Arts
    and Sciences

224

SHIP RESTORATIONS AND REPLICAS

CANADA
Vancouver (Vancouver Maritime
  Museum)
  R.C.M.P. *St Roch,* restoration of
    police schooner. Made the
    first voyage through Northwest
    Passage from west to east,
    and first ship to
    circumnavigate North
    America
Dawson, Yukon Territory
  Restored stern-wheeler,
    SS *Keno*

GREAT BRITAIN
Bristol
  SS *Great Britain,* first
    propellor-driven ocean liner,
    launched 19 July 1843 and
    made her first transatlantic
    voyage from Liverpool to
    New York in 1845. Storage
    hulk at Falkland Islands
    1866 to 1970, when she was
    salvaged, towed back to
    Bristol and restored

Castletown, Isle of Man
  Schooner-rigged yacht *Peggy,*
    built 1791 and oldest surviving
    vessel of her type
Dundee, Angus, Scotland
  HMS *Unicorn,* 150ft, 46-gun
    frigate built 1824 and
    believed to be fourth oldest
    ship afloat
Greenwich, London SE10
  Clipper ship *Cutty Sark,*
    launched Dumbarton 1869
    and participant in China tea
    and Australian wool trades.
    On board is a collection of
    figureheads
  Gipsy Moth IV, 54ft ketch in
    which Sir Francis Chichester
    made his epic single-handed
    circumnavigation of the
    world, 29,000 miles in 226
    days
Great Yarmouth, Norfolk
  Broads racing lateener, built c.
    1827

Isle of Wight
  Paddle steamer *Medway Queen*
London, Victoria Embankment
  Discovery, Capt Scott's Antarctic
    expedition ship
  HMS *President*, formerly the
    Saxifrage, built in 1918 and
    fitted out as a Q-boat for
    World War I
  HMS *Belfast*, last cruiser of her
    type afloat
Portsmouth, Hampshire
  HMS *Victory*, restoration of Lord
    Nelson's flagship, a 1st rate,
    186 x 52ft, built at Chatham
    in 1765
  HMS *Foudroyant*, a frigate built
    in 1817
Lower Upnor, Hampshire
  Arethusa (ex-*Peking*) School
    ship, built 1911
Newcastle-upon-Tyne
  SS *Turbinia*, world's first
    turbine-engined ship, 100ft
    in length, 44½ tons, built
    in 1894 and attained a speed of
    31 knots in 1897
Sea Houses, Northumberland
  Grace Darling's coble
Plymouth, Devon
  Kathleen & May, wooden
    three-masted topsail trading
    schooner launched in 1900 as
    the *Lizzie May* and last
    surviving example of her type
Rochester, Kent
  Cambria, last unaltered Thames
    sailing barge and last ship on
    British Register to trade
    under sail alone
Windermere, Westmoreland
  Dolly, Ullswater steam
    pleasure craft built in 1850,

now restored by Windemere
  Nautical Trust
Glasgow
  Carrick, ex-*City of Adelaide*,
    clipper ship built in 1864
Leith
  Dolphin, barque built in 1883
    and now used as training ship

SWEDEN
Lyngby
  S.S. *Skelskør*, coastal passenger
    vessel
Stockholm
  Warship *Wasa*, sunk in 1628.
    Salvaged, restored and put
    on display in 1962

SWITZERLAND
Lucerne (Swiss Transport
  Museum)
  Rigi, 1847 steamship

UNITED STATES
Alabama
Mobile
  Battleship U.S.S. *Alabama*
California
Long Beach
  Passenger liner *Queen Mary*
San Diego
  Sailing ship *Star of India*
San Francisco (San Francisco
  Maritime Museum)
  British merchant ship
    Balclutha and side-wheeler
    Eppleton Hall
San Francisco (San Francisco
  Maritime State Historic Park)
  Scow schooner *Alma*, lumber
    schooner *C. A. Thayer*,
    steam schooner *Wapama*,
    paddle-wheel ferry *Eureka*

Connecticut

Groton
Ferry *Jamestown*
Mystic (Mystic Seaport)
Whaling vessel *Charles W. Morgan*, square-rigged training vessel *Joseph Conrad*, fishing schooner *L. A. Dutton*

District of Columbia (Smithsonian Institution)
Gunboat *Philadelphia*

Florida

St Petersburg
Bounty, replica of Captain Bligh's ship, used for movie *Mutiny on the Bounty*

Iowa

Keokuk (Keokuk River Museum)
Mississippi River steamboat *George M. Verity*

Maine

Bath (Bath Maritime Museum)
Schooner *Isaac H. Evans*
Boothbay Harbor
Steamtug *Seguin*; fishing schooner *Sherman Zwicker*

Maryland

Baltimore
Frigate *Constellation*

Massachusetts

Boston
U.S.S. *Constitution*
Fall River
Battleship U.S.S. *Massachusetts*
Plymouth
Mayflower II, replica

Michigan

Douglas
Steamship S.S. *Keewatin*
Sault Ste. Marie
Great Lakes freighter *Valley Camp*

Minnesota

Winona
Stern-wheeler *Julius C. Wilkie*

Missouri

St Louis
U.S.S. *Inaugural*, warship

New York

New York City (South Street Seaport Museum)
Wavertree, iron-hulled sailing ship; *Alexander Hamilton*, paddle-wheel steamer; *Moshulu*, four-masted bark; other vessels still under restoration
Sag Harbor (Suffolk County Whaling Museum)
American whaleboat

North Carolina

Wilmington
U.S.S. *North Carolina*, warship

Ohio

Marietta
Steamer *W. P. Snyder, Jr.*

Oregon

Astoria (Columbia River Maritime Museum)
Lightship No. 88, *Columbia*

Pennsylvania

Erie
U.S.S. *Niagara*, sailing warship
Philadelphia (Philadelphia Maritime Museum)
Barkentine *Gazela Primeiro*, U.S.S. *Olympia*

Rhode Island

Newport
Revolutionary War frigate H.M.S. *Rose*

Texas

Galveston
Submarine U.S.S. *Cavella*

Houston
   Battleship *Texas*
Vermont
Shelburne (Shelburne Museum)
   S.S. *Ticonderoga*
Virginia
Jamestown
   Susan Constant, Godspeed and
   Discovery, replicas of sailing
   ships

Washington
Seattle (Northwest Seaport)
   Sailing schooner *Wawona*, tug
   Arthur Foss (formerly the
   Wallowa), lightship *Relief*,
   submarine *Bowfin*, steam
   ferry *San Mateo*
Wisconsin
Manitowoc (Manitowoc Maritime
   Museum)
   Submarine *Cobia*

BIBLIOGRAPHY

BOOKS

Albian, Robert Greenhalgh. *Naval and Maritime History, An Annotated Bibliography.* Newton Abbot, Devon, England: David & Charles Ltd., 1972.

Banks, Steven. *The Handicrafts of the Sailor.* Newton Abbot, Devon, England: David & Charles Ltd., 1974.

Barnes, Clare, Jr. *John F. Kennedy, Scrimshaw Collector.* Boston and Toronto: Little, Brown & Co., 1964.

Bedford, John. *The Collecting Man.* New York: David McKay Co., Inc., 1968.

Bennett, Geoffrey. *Nelson the Commander.* New York: Charles Scribner's Sons, 1972.

Body, Geoffrey. *British Paddle Steamers.* Newton Abbot, Devon, England: David & Charles Ltd., 1974.

Brock, P. W. and Greenhill, Basil. *Steam and Sail in Britain and North America.* Newton Abbot, Devon, England: David & Charles Ltd., 1973.

Canter, Clive. *Cornish Shipwrecks: The North Coast.* Newton Abbot, Devon, England: David & Charles Ltd., 1970.

Christensen, Erwin O. *The Index of American Design.* New York: The Macmillan Co. Washington: National Gallery of Art, 1950.

Colledge, J. *Ships of the Royal Navy: An Historical Index*, 2 vols. Newton Abbot, Devon, England: David & Charles Ltd., 1969 and 1970.

Cousteau, Jacques-Yves, and Diolé, Philippe. *Diving for Sunken Treasure.* Garden City, N.Y.: Doubleday & Co., Inc., 1971.

Cutler, Carl C. *Greyhounds of the Sea.* New York: Halcyon House, 1970.

Dao, G. F. *Whale Ships and Whaling During Three Centuries*. Salem, Mass.: 1935.

Dunn, Lawrence. *The Book of Ships*. Gothenburg, Sweden: Tre Tryckare, Cagner & Co., 1968.

Earle, Walter K. *Scrimshaw, Folk Art of the Whalers*. Cold Spring Harbor, New York: Whaling Museum Society, Inc., 1957.

Farbrother, Robina. *Ships*. London: Paul Hamlyn, Ltd., 1963.

Flayderman, E. Norman. *Scrimshaw and Scrimshanders, Whales and Whalemen*. New Milford, Connecticut: N. Flayderman & Co., 1972.

Forbes, Allan, and Eastman, Ralph M. *Other Yankee Ship Sailing Cards*. Boston: State Street Trust Co., 1949.

Forbes, Allan, and Eastman, Ralph M. *Yankee Ship Sailing Cards*. Boston: State Street Trust Co., 1948.

Frére-Cook, Gervis, editor. *The Decorative Arts of the Mariner*. Boston and Toronto: Little, Brown, & Co., 1966. London: Cassell & Co., Ltd., 1966.

Godden, Geoffrey A. *An Illustrated Encyclopedia of British Pottery and Porcelain*. New York, Crown Publishers, Inc., 1966.

Godden, Geoffrey A. *British Pottery and Porcelain, 1780–1850*. Cranbury, New Jersey: A. S. Barnes & Co., Inc., 1964.

Greene, Richard Lawrence, and Wheeling, Kenneth Edward. *A Pictorial History of the Shelburne Museum*. Shelburne, Vermont: Shelburne Museum, Inc., 1972.

Greenhill, Basil. *The Merchant Schooners*, 2 vols. Newton Abbot, Devon, England: David & Charles Ltd., revised 1968.

Guldbeck, Per E. *The Care of Historical Collections: A Conservation Handbook for the Nonspecialist*. Nashville, Tennessee: American Association for State and Local History, 1972.

Guttridge, Leonard F., and Smith, Jay D. *The Commodores: The U. S. Navy in the Age of Sail*. New York: Harper & Row, 1969.

Hansen, Hans Jurgen, general editor. *Art and the Seafarer: A Historical Survey of the Arts and Crafts of Sailors and Shipwrights*. New York: The Viking Press, 1968.

Harbottle, Thomas. *Dictionary of Battles*. New York: Stein and Day, 1971.

Holland, Rupert Sargent. *Historic Ships*. Philadelphia: Macrae Smith Co., 1926.

Hornung, Clarence P. *Treasury of American Design*. New York: Harry N. Abrams, Inc., 1972.

Howse, Denck and Sanderson, Michael. *The Sea Chart*. Newton Abbot, Devon, England: David & Charles Ltd., 1973.

Hubbard, Donald. *Ships in Bottles*. Newton Abbot, Devon, England: David & Charles Ltd., 1973.

Hughes, G. Bernard. *Victorian Pottery and Porcelain*. New York: The Macmillan Co., 1959.

Jourdain, Margaret, and Jenyns, R. Soams. *Chinese Export Art in the Eighteenth Century*. Middlesex: Spring Books, 1967.

Kemp, Peter. *History of the Royal Navy*. New York: G. P. Putnam's Sons, 1969.

Kihlberg, Bengt, supervising editor. *The Lore of Ships*. Stockholm, Sweden: Tre Tryckare. New York: Holt, Rinehart & Winston, 1963.

Larn, Richard. *Cornish Shipwrecks: The Isles of Scilly*. Newton Abbot, Devon, England: David & Charles Ltd., 1971.

Larn, Richard. *Devon Shipwrecks*. Newton Abbot, Devon, England: David & Charles Ltd., 1974.

Larn, Richard and Canter, Clive. *Cornish Shipwrecks: The South Coast*. Newton Abbot, Devon, England: David & Charles Ltd., 1969.

Lewis, Edward V., O'Brien, Robert, and the Editors of *Life*. *Ships*. New York: Time, Inc., 1965.

Locher, Harry O., editor. *Waterways of the United States: Rivers, Harbors, Lakes, Canals*. New York: The National Association of River and Harbor Contractors, 1963.

Lyon, Jane D. *Clipper Ships and Captains*. New York: American Heritage Publishing Co., Inc., 1962.

Macintyre, Donald, and Bathe, Basil W. *Man-of-War: A History of the Combat Vessel*. New York, Toronto: McGraw-Hill Book Co., 1969.

Mahan, A. T. *The Influence of Sea Power Upon History*. Boston: Little, Brown & Co., 1925.

Marran, Ray J. *Making Models of Famous Ships*. New York, London: D. Appleton-Century Co., 1940.

Marx, Robert F. *Shipwrecks of the Western Hemisphere, 1492–1825*. New York: The World Publishing Co., 1971.

Matthews, Leonard Harrison, and others. *The Whale*. New York: Simon & Schuster, Inc. 1968.

Paine, Ralph D. *The Ships and Sailors of Old Salem*. New York: The Outing Publishing Co., 1908.

Pearsall, Ronald. *Collecting and Restoring Scientific Instruments*. Newton Abbot, Devon, England: David & Charles Ltd., 1974.

Pope, Dudley. *The Great Gamble: Nelson at Copenhagen*. New York: Simon & Schuster, Inc., 1972.

Popular Science Monthly Editorial Staff. *Manual of Ship Model Making*. New York: Popular Science Publishing Co., 1934.

Ringwald, Donald C. *Hudson River Day Line: The Story of a Great American Steamboat Company*. Berkeley, California: Howell-North Books, 1965.

231

Rogers, Stanley. *The Atlantic*. London, George Harrap & Co. Ltd., 1930 and New York: Thomas Y. Crowell, 1938.

Rowland, K. T. *The "Great Britain."* Newton Abbot, Devon, England: David & Charles, Ltd., 1971.

Smellie, K. B. *Great Britain Since 1688*. Ann Arbor, Michigan: University of Michigan Press, 1962.

Stackpole, Edouard A. *Figureheads and Ship Carvings at Mystic Seaport*. Mystic, Connecticut: The Marine Historical Association, Inc., 1964.

Sténuit, Robert. *Treasures of the Armada*. Newton Abbot, Devon, England: David & Charles Ltd., 1972.

Villiers, Alan. *The Way of a Ship*. New York: Charles Scribner's Sons, 1970.

Warner, Oliver. *Nelson's Battles*. Newton Abbot, Devon, England: David & Charles Ltd., 2nd imp. 1971.

White, R. J. *The Horizon Concise History of England*. New York: American Heritage Publishing Co., 1971.

Whiting, J. *Commemorative Medals*. Newton Abbot, Devon, England: David & Charles Ltd., 1972.

Wilkes, Bill St. John. *Nautical Archaeology: A Handbook*. Newton Abbot, Devon, England: David & Charles Ltd., 1971.

Wynne-Jones, Ivor. *Shipwrecks of North Wales*. Newton Abbot, Devon, England: David & Charles Ltd., 1973.

PERIODICALS

Barbeau, Marius. "Seafaring Folk Art." *Antiques*, July, 1954.

Barnes, Clare, and Bowen, Croswell. "The Scrimshaw Collector." *American Heritage*, vol. 15, no. 6. October, 1964.

Carroll, Dana H. "Little Ships." *Century Magazine*, August, 1911.

Haze, Wellington. "Jagging Wheels." *Antiques*, June, 1922.

Hustern, H. Harrison. "Scrimshaw: One Part Whalebone, Two Parts Nostalgia." *Antiques*, August, 1961.

Robotti, Frances Diane. "Scrimshaw, the Whaleman's Art." *Antiques Journal*, March, 1965.

Wilson, Claggett. "Scrimshaw, The Whaleman's Art." *Antiques*, November, 1944.

CATALOGS (Auction, Museum and Commercial)

Alwilda Presents Nautical Relics: Gifts From the Sea. A Naval and Marine Collection. The Anderson Galleries, New York, 25 and 26 March, 1923.

Important Ship Models. Marine Paintings and Relics. The Anderson Galleries, New York, 11 December, 1924.

Flayderman, N. *Military and Nautical Antiquities,* Catalog 92. N. Flayderman & Co., Inc., 1973.

An Outstanding Whaling Auction. Louis Joseph Auction Galleries, Inc.,
18 November, 1972.

The American Heritage Society Auction of Americana. Parke-Bernet
Galleries, New York, 12 and 13 November 1971.

The Marine Room of the Peabody Museum of Salem. Peabody Museum,
Salem, Massachusetts, 1921.

*Catalogue of Fine English Furniture, Ship Models, Tapestries and Tex-
tiles.* Sotheby & Co., London, 2 April 1971.

Valhalla: Maritime Museum at Tresco. Isles of Scilly, no date.

INDEX

237

241